Kesey's Jail Journal

Kesey's Jail Journal

Cut the M*********** Loose

Ken Kesey

Introduction by Ed McClanahan

Viking

VIKING
Published by the Penguin Group
Penguin Group (USA) Inc., 375 Hudson Street, New York, New York 10014, U.S.A.
Penguin Books Ltd, 80 Strand, London WC2R 0RL, England
Penguin Books Australia Ltd, 250 Camberwell Road, Camberwell, Victoria 3124, Australia
Penguin Books Canada Ltd, 10 Alcorn Avenue, Toronto, Ontario, Canada M4V 3B2
Penguin Books India (P) Ltd, 11 Community Centre, Panchsheel Park, New Delhi – 110 017, India
Penguin Books (N.Z.) Ltd, Cnr Rosedale and Airborne Roads, Albany, Auckland, New Zealand
Penguin Books (South Africa) (Pty) Ltd, 24 Sturdee Avenue, Rosebank, Johannesburg 2196, South Africa

Penguin Books Ltd, Registered Offices: 80 Strand, London WC2R 0RL, England

First published in 2003 by Viking Penguin, a member of Penguin Group (USA) Inc.

1 3 5 7 9 10 8 6 4 2

Copyright © Kesey, L.L.C., 2003
Introduction copyright © Ed McClanahan, 2003
All rights reserved

LIBRARY OF CONGRESS CATALOGING-IN-PUBLICATION DATA
Kesey, Ken
[Jail journal]
Kesey's jail journal : cut the m*********** loose / Ken Kesey ;
introduction by Ed McClanahan.
p. cm.
ISBN 0-670-87693-3 (alk. paper)
1. Kesey, Ken—Diaries. 2. Authors, American—20th century—Diaries.
3. Prisoners—California—San Mateo—Diaries. I. Title: Jail journal. II. McClanahan, Ed. III. Title.

PS3561.E667Z7 2003   818.5403—dc21   [B]
2003047968

Printed in the United Kingdom
Designed by Jaye Zimet

Contents

Editor's Note

Ken Kesey began this project in 1967, filling 8" x 10" notebooks with art and writing while serving time in the San Mateo County Jail and the Sheriff's Honor Camp. Upon his release he returned home to Oregon, and in an intense period of work collaged together text and art from the jail notebooks with additional material, creating dozens of elaborately illustrated 18" x 23" pages. Upon realizing that this ambitious book's intended format involved then-insurmountable publishing difficulties, he set the project aside. In 1997 he returned to it, and signed a contract with his longtime publisher, Viking.

At that point Kesey's intent was to present each intricate art page in color on a right-hand page, with a facing page mimicking its layout in type-only form. The reader could thus choose between an express lane read-through on one side, and a complete, scenic, sometimes labyrinthine, words-and-art journey on the other. But as Kesey reimmersed himself in the material he began to expand the text, eventually taking it well beyond what it had been in the art page version. Certain gaps and anomalies of chronology were addressed as he elaborated on some sections, worked in additional entries taken from the original notebooks, added letters, and developed and renamed some of the characters.

Progress on the book was interrupted by other projects—the musical *Twister,* the play *Where'sMerlin?* (performed in 1999 during a month-long bus run through England, Wales, Ireland, and Scotland), and the editing of the first two installments of the 1964 bus movie *Intrepid Traveler and His Merry Band of Pranksters Look for a Kool Place*— but Kesey returned to it numerous times until shortly before his death. There is no question that he wanted to take it much further. But as Mark Levine noted, "Nothing more is nothing less."

—David Stanford

Cut 'em Loose!

an introduction by Ed McClanahan

In early November 2001, while Ken Kesey lay dying in an Oregon hospital, I was talking to his brother Chuck about the possibility that he might pull through somehow. Taking the optimistic view, I told Chuck about a little incident that had happened several years earlier, when I was visiting Ken just after a stroke had left his right arm and hand temporarily paralyzed. Ken was attempting to pick up a small piece of paper off the desk in his office, and his hand was refusing to cooperate.

"C'mon, hand!" he commanded the offending extremity. "Work!"

"And sure enough," I told Chuck, "his hand grabbed up that slip of paper so fast you could almost hear the hand squeak, 'Okay, boss! Okay!' So I think if anybody could *will* himself to get well again, it'd be Ken."

"Well, I don't think that's what's happening," Chuck said. "I think he's lookin' down that long, dark tunnel, and he sees that bright little light down there, and now he's headed for it."

That would be like him, I had to admit. That would be very, very like him.

Ken Kesey. Author of a novel (*One Flew Over the Cuckoo's Nest*) which profoundly affected the consciousness of a generation, psychedelic mover and shaker, acid paladin, cosmic iconoclast, hero of yet another book (Tom Wolfe's *The Electric Kool-Aid Acid Test*) which profoundly affected the consciousness of a generation . . .

Okay, let me remind you.

In 1962, Kesey—former University of Oregon championship heavyweight wrestler, former graduate student in Wallace Stegner's and Malcolm Cowley's seminars in Stegner's famous Creative Writing Center at Stanford University, and former subject in one of the earliest paid-volunteer, CIA-sponsored research experiments with psychotropic drugs—published his landmark *Cuckoo's Nest,* the novel that many believe launched the counter-cultural revolution of the Day-Glo Decade. He followed up in 1964 with the epic *Sometimes a Great Notion* (which, though it drew mixed reviews, is perhaps the greater of the two books), and seemed well on his way to a long career as a novelist.

Never trust a Prankster. In the summer of 1964, Ken incorporated himself (Intrepid Trips, Inc.), purchased a 1939 International schoolbus, an Aeroflex camera and other serious moviemaking gear, gathered about him at his La Honda, California, home a group of old and new friends (over the next several years their number would fluctuate from as high as thirty down to half a dozen hardy souls), set them to work preparing the bus for the caper he was planning (the preparations largely consisted of finger-painting its aged yellow fuse-lage in an infinite variety of colors), hollered the equivalent of "All ashore that's going ashore!" (about fifteen people weren't), and struck out for the New York World's Fair, with the intention of making, along the way, a film rather cumbrously entitled *Intrepid Traveler and His Merry Band of Pranksters Look for a Kool Place.*

It turned out to be arguably the longest, strangest trip that's ever been, an odyssey which delivered to an unprepared America its first national contact high, and which, it might be said, resolutely proceeds apace to this very day. The bus—"FURTHER," read the manifest—piloted by Beat Generation icon Neal Cassady, meandered across the country outraging local sensibilities at every opportunity and raising consciousness at a prodigious rate, to such an extent that the whole escapade captured the national attention and Kesey's fame as a novelist began to be subsumed by his notoriety as a cultural phenomenon.

Two months later, Kesey and the Pranksters were back in La Honda with thirty-six hours of 16-millimeter color film of their adventures, which they intended to edit down to a feature-length movie. They set up a cutting room in a shed in Kesey's yard, and in April 1965, they were still editing away (the Keseys' 1964 Christmas tree had been decorated with about half a mile of cut film) when the sheriff of San Mateo County and his merry band of deputies swept down and arrested Kesey and thirteen of the Pranksters for possession of marijuana. All were released on bail the following day, and the charges against twelve of the fourteen were soon dropped; but in December, Kesey and one other Prankster—Page Browning, a longtime friend—were convicted, sentenced to six months in jail and three years of probation, then released on appeal.

During the seven-month interim between the arrest and the conviction, Kesey and the Pranksters, along with the then-unknown rock band that became known as the Grateful Dead, had begun to produce a series of psychedelically enhanced Saturday night happenings they called "The Acid Test." As word spread, ever-larger crowds turned out for these public events, which were held at various Bay Area venues.

On the weekend following Kesey's conviction, the Acid Test was scheduled to be the main attraction of a three-day marathon psychedelic circus called the Trips Festival (the promoters were Kesey, *Whole Earth Catalog* publisher Stewart Brand, and rock impresario Bill Graham) which would be held in the vast, big-top-like Longshoremen's Hall on Fisherman's Wharf. Many unheralded Bay Area rock groups signed up to perform—among them the Quicksilver Messenger Service, the Charlatans, Big Brother and the Holding Company (with their bluesy, blowzy young singer Janis Joplin), and, of course, the Grateful Dead—and there would also be throbbing-blob light shows, the San Francisco Mime Troupe, a Stewart Brand slide show called "America Needs Indians," and, topping the bill, Ken Kesey's Acid Test.

Five nights before the Trips Festival was to open, Kesey was arrested again, this time on a San Francisco rooftop in the company of a nineteen-year-old Prankster named Carolyn "Mountain Girl" Adams . . . and a small quantity of marijuana.

Kesey, once again free on bail, did participate in the Trips Festival, which was a huge success. An estimated 12,000 subterranean freaks, heads, Bohos, and retro-Beats crept out of their cribs and digs and pads into the light and found to their amazement that there were

11,999 other freaks, *just like themselves,* in town. Presto! In the blink of a weekend, a brand-new community discovers itself and instantly becomes a major force in the city's political and cultural life. By defining and energizing it, the Trips Festival may be said to have begat the entire fledgling San Francisco psychedelic rock scene—the Fillmore Auditorium (Bill Graham's principal venue), Winterland, Chet Helms's Family Dog, the Avalon Ballroom, and half a dozen smaller Bay Area hotspots—which in turn spawned Life As We Know It. And Ken Kesey had won a permanent place in the embryonic history of rock 'n' roll, not in the usual way (though in fact the Pranksters once formed their own rock group and cut an unforgettably dubious LP) but as the inventor of a whole new way to listen.

Within a week after the festival, an elderly truck registered to Kesey and containing a pair of fluorescent sneakers (a Kesey trademark) and a suicide note ("Ocean, ocean, I'll beat you in the end . . . ") was found parked atop a cliff above the sea along a lonely stretch of the northern California coast. And Ken Kesey, disguised as "mild-mannered reporter Steve Lamb," was in sunny Puerto Vallarta, Mexico, knockin' back the margaritas.

There he remained for almost two months, until he attempted to phone his wife, Faye, in California, and a well-intentioned friend inadvertently mentioned the call in the presence of a *real* newspaper reporter. "Kesey the Corpse Having a Ball!" screamed the next day's headlines. Friends frantically wired him that the jig was up, and after hiding out in the Puerto Vallarta jungle for several days he made his way south to Manzanillo, a tropical beach resort rarely visited by gringo tourists. Meanwhile, the Texas novelist Larry McMurtry (Kesey's close friend since their student days at Stanford) had arranged, through a Mexico City attorney, for Kesey to be granted a temporary and somewhat shaky amnesty by the local Colima government. Within weeks a small coterie of Pranksters had arrived, bus and all, followed shortly by Faye and the three Kesey children. They set up shop in a house on the Manzanillo beach and began again to work on the film, which by this time was nearly fifty hours long and seemed to be growing faster than the editing process could manage to shrink it.

Kesey remained in Manzanillo for the next six months, an idyll frequently shattered by the sometimes real, sometimes imagined threat of Federales, "FBEyes," or vacationing deputies from the San Mateo County sheriff's office. In the fall of 1966, Kesey returned to the States, this time crossing the border on a borrowed horse, carrying a guitar and calling himself "Singin' Jimmy Anglund." He hid out for nearly two weeks in the homes of Bay Area friends, granted interviews to trusted newspaper and TV reporters, and "rubbed salt in J. Edgar Hoover's wounds" until half a dozen FBI agents in a carpool chanced to spot him in stop-and-go traffic on the Bayshore Freeway, gave chase, and got their man at last.

Kesey was released within a few days, after several of his friends put up their homes to make his bail. He was then tried on the San Francisco charge, and convicted of a misdemeanor ("knowingly being in a place where marijuana is possessed"). In the meantime, his San Mateo County appeal had failed, and on June 23, 1967, he and Page Browning entered the San Mateo County jail and were shortly thereafter transferred to the Sheriff's Honor

Camp (a facility located in the coastal redwood country almost literally a stone's throw from Kesey's own La Honda backyard) to serve out their old six-month sentences.

Every two or three Sundays during those months, my first wife, Kit, and I would pack up our three kids and a picnic basket and drive up to the Honor Camp to have a picnic lunch with the yardbirds. The first time we went, Kit took Ken a stash of art supplies she'd picked out, including a set of Day-Glo pens. And on our second visit, he showed up with the first few pages of this luminous illuminated manuscript (imagine here a monk in his cell . . . a cell with bars!) called *Cut the Motherfuckers Loose,* an illustrated journal of the incarceration he was currently enjoying.

It came as no surprise to me that Ken could draw (years before, I'd seen a batch of his razor-sharp sketches of the characters in *Cuckoo's Nest*) or that he had a great pop-aesthetic sense of color and design (the bus itself testified to that). What was astonishing, though, as we saw more and more of these pages on subsequent visits, was that he could sustain such a high level of intensity, page after page after page, each so crammed with words and colors and faces and forms that it seemed ready to explode in your face like a letter bomb. For a jail, the Sheriff's Honor Camp was relatively humane, but as one might suppose, confinement chafed and galled Ken even more than it would most people, and therefore capital-C Confinement is an almost palpable evil presence in the journal, just as all those words and images and colors seem to be in constant struggle against the edges of the page. The text, with its antic spellings and deliberate crudities and fragments of pin-up porn, is like runic scribblings on the jailhouse wall: cramped, volatile, funny, and as conspiratorial as a jail-break.

After his release, Ken beat a strategic retreat to Oregon, and he and Faye set up house-keeping in an old dairy barn on a small farm near Springfield, where Faye still lives today. In late 1967, a few pages of Kesey's jail journals appeared in *Ramparts* magazine, reduced to the size of playing cards, in "color" but, compared to the originals, looking as muddy and murky as if they'd been dipped in bongwater.

Up in Oregon, Ken spent the next several months working on the jail journal, with an eye to publishing it in book form, until it became apparent that print technology as it existed at that time simply wasn't capable of doing justice to this oversized, illustrated work. He reluctantly abandoned the project, and the finished pages eventually landed in the Special Collections room of the University of Oregon, which has extensive holdings of Ken's papers. Meanwhile, the bus trip film was proving stubbornly resistant to all attempts to cut it down to size, and it too was eventually shelved.

In the mid-1990s, modern technology came to the rescue of the 1964 movie when the new, computerized Avid editing machine made it possible at last to transfer all that old film footage to videotape, edit it, and synchronize the sound. Kesey, his longtime friend and cohort Ken Babbs, and a couple of techno-savvy second-generation Pranksters completed two hour-long videos (a third is in the works) and made them available on the Prankster website (www.intrepidtrips.com).

During the thirty-odd years after his return to Oregon, Kesey had published many books—autobiographical essays, cultural commentary, children's books, a wonderful grab-bag miscellany called *Garage Sale,* even another novel or two, as well as six issues of an extraordinary little magazine, *Spit in the Ocean.* But the fabled jail book languished in an archival box on a shelf in the library until, *mirabile dictu,* it happened again: new technology rode to the rescue and made possible the remarkable volume you now hold before you.

But way back in 1990 there had transpired the first of these miraculous resuscitations, this time of Further itself. Actually, the original Further—the Ur-Further, I like to call it—was long since beyond saving, so Ken had retired it to the swamp behind the barn. He bought himself a ringer, a compact '49 International bus in good running order, and turned it into the sweetest little article of psychedelic rolling stock that ever toddled down the pike.

Fittingly, when Ken died eleven years later, the renascent Further bore him in grand style to his grave.

Kesey's Jail Journal

CUT THE MOTHERFUCKERS LOOSE

ONE DAY I'm

SITTING OUTSIDE THE ~~Tart~~ TAILOR SHOP...
got my shirt off, belly to the afternoon sun,
listening to Bud Shank jap flute music drift
into the Redwoods... painstakingly darning socks
pulled over a light bulb... mellowed by a little
hit off the ball of opium Ramrod and Gasgirl
smuggled in the other night... listening, stitching,
doing good Oriental type job on each sock...
when **DEPUTY MOLINARI** drops
by and pulls himself up a chair for a little
~~sincerity~~ and ~~man~~-to-~~man~~ business:

"Kesey... I been wanting a chance to talk with
you... our celebrity." TIK TIK TIK ... DUM DE DUM — DUM

"Sure." I turn down the music, sit back
down, continue stitching. Molinari's about 35,
thin, a good hunter and a dedicated policeman.
His face is a mask of humanitarianism worn
mighty thin about the eyes as a result of being
burned so many times by those he had
thought rehibilitated. A pretty good guy if he
~~wal~~ would shed the mask and get back to
the soul that put it on in its first place. But
once burned and so forth. We talk about the

"SOME PEOPLE REHABILITATE EASIER THAN OTHERS."
(HENRY VIII)

usual cop-Kesey stuff: my writing... to why I quit
... to dope... to why I don't got. He advances some
of his theories about the **MOVEMENT**. I counter
with some of mine. Fairly straight bullshit, no
truth but obvious to both of us that we are truthfully trying to get some thing going. Then, off
the wall, he stops me and asks:

"ARE you loaded?"
I think it was more my ideas than my
manner that prompted the question. Because I was
sitting ~~fast~~ fairly cool. You can be extremely cool
when you're high in a jail situation: you're clean,
you're high, and you don't have to worry about being
caught. I thought, maybe my eyes; I don't know
much about opium and ~~my~~ maybe my eyes are
dialated... So I picked my shirt up and
removed my colored glasses from the pocket
slowly, smiling at his waiting mask of the
Burned Good Guy.

"Mr. Molinari," I answered, ceremoniously
adjusting my shades; "Allow me to make one
thing clear before we continue our conversation...
I'll lie to you."

SLAM

June 23 —— D-day
We're in. So I guess D could stand
for defeat. Except to such a trip.
Bus, Pranksters, Faye, kids, everybody
in that courtroom doing the courtroom
zonk blah blah blah then suddenly
very fast and efficient we're standing
up and the judge is finished and (here
it gets weird) moving out of that
same old stiff agonizing courtroom
posture (here we start to come out
of the zonk) walking through the
double doors only this time everybody is
turning left toward the elevator except

SLAM

Cut the Motherfuckers Loose

One day (<u>been at San Mateo Sheriff's Honor Camp coupla months, long enough to be appointed camp tailor</u>) I'm sitting outside the tailor shop . . . got my shirt off, belly to the afternoon sun, listening to my Bud Shank longplay Jap flute music drift into the redwoods . . . painstakingly darning a sock pulled over a lightbulb . . . mellowed by a little hit of the ball of O that Ramrod and Gasgirl smuggled in the other night . . . listening, stitching, doing a good Oriental type job on each sock . . . when Deputy Rhack drops by and pulls himself up a chair for a little sincerity and man-to-man business:

"Kesey . . . I been wanting a chance to talk to you . . . our celebrity." Tik Tik Tik . . . DUM DE DUM-DUM.

"Sure." I turn down the music, sit back down, continue stitching. Rhack's about 35, thin, a deer hunter and dedicated policeman. His face is a mask of humanitarianism worn mighty thin about the eyes as a result of being burned so many times by all those ingrates he thought he had <u>rehabilitated</u>.

> ("Some people rehabilitate
> easier than others."— Henry VIII)

A pretty good guy, Rhack . . . if he would shed the mask and get back to the soul that put it on in the first place. But once burned and so forth. We chat about the usual cop–Kesey stuff: my writing . . . to why I quit . . . to dope . . . to why I <u>don't</u> quit. He advances some of his theories about the MOVEMENT (psychedelic, that is). I counter with some of mine. Fairly straight bullshit, no truth but obvious to both of us that we are truthfully trying to get <u>something</u> going. Then, off the wall, he cuts off the chat and asks:

"Are you loaded?"

I think it was more my ideas than my manner that prompted the question. Because I was sitting fairly cool. You can be extremely cool when you're high in a jail situation: you're clean, you're loaded, and you don't have to worry about being caught. I also thought, maybe my eyes? I don't know much about O and maybe my eyes are dilated?

He's still studying me hard, so I pick my shirt up and remove my colored glasses from the pocket, slowly, smiling at his waiting mask of The-Good-Guy-Burned-By-Too-Many-Bad-Guys-Too-Many-Times.

"Mr. Rhack," I answer, ceremoniously adjusting my shades; "Allow me to make one thing clear before we continue our conversation . . . I'll lie to you."

SLAM!

Incarceration begins, June 23, 1967—"D" day.

Page and I are in so I guess in our situation "D" should stand for defeat. Except it's all been such a trip—Bus, Pranksters, Faye, kids, everybody in that courtroom doing the courtroom zonk blah blah blah then suddenly very fast and efficient we're standing up and the judge is finished and (and here it gets weird) moving out of that same old stiff agonizing courtroom posture (here we start to come out of the zonk) walking through the double doors only this time everybody is turning left toward the elevator except Page and me (here we begin to believe it) hustled away from our people too fast for attempted farewells (yep, now we believe it) upstairs prints photos clothes "B Tank, boys." Ka-slash! Door slides open. Ka-slam! shut . . . Then we're grinning at each other, Page and I, the pair left out of the 14 of us busted almost two years ago. Page Browning (alias Dez Prado) (the one person I am definitely never to associate with according to the terms of my probation) and me (alias Tarnished Galahad) . . . grinning at each other in a cement box along with some other guys.

We climb onto our bunks. Still grinning. Hear the big gate down the corridor shut. KashlAM!

"Hap'nin," says Page.

Dear Faye:

First thing that sticks is Lord, what dreams! Last night cranked out some super weird sleepmares (get them night or day understand?) that I woulda never believed my skull capable of containing. Twisted, sick, stark dreams. All in black and white. Belladonna bummers all of them, revolving around a child molesting theme: You reckon a man gotta get himself locked up to free that kind of crap lodged in the crannies of his cranium?

I've put in a request to get in the kitchen. Get out of this low rent B Tank do a little dish washing, maybe tire myself into a decent sleep. Also put in to go before the board that picks men for the honor camp up on Skyline. That's up there so close to La Honda almost like going home—luv, Ken

DREAMS DREAMS SO WEIRD AND FIERCE That I think for a while they are PROVOKED BY THE BROTHERS IN OUR CELL . . .

—first time you know I've actually lived with blacks. And by golly you know? they are different.

And I spend a lot of time thinking about *Heart of Darkness.*
. . . Until I watch long enough and get close enough to see "different," yes; but it's my

Page and I (here we all begin to
believe it) hustled away from our people
too fast for attempted farewells (yep, now
we believe it) upstairs print, photos clothes
"B Tank, boys." Ka-slash! Door slide
open. Ka-slam! shut... Then we're grinning
at each other, Page and I, the two left
out of the 14 busted almost 2 years ago.
Page Browning alias Dez Prado, the one
person I am definately never to associate
with according to the term of my probation,
and I...grinning at each other in a
cement box along with some other guys.
   We climb onto our bunks. Still
grinning. Hear the big gate down the
corridor slide shut. KachBAM!
   "Hap'nin," says Page.

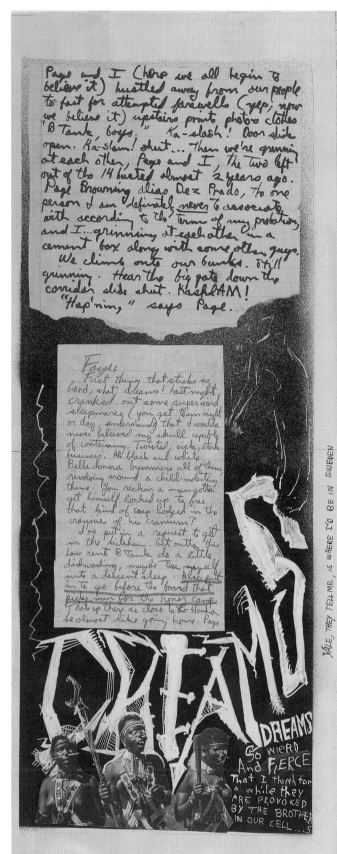

Page:
   First thing that sticks is,
Lord, what dreams! Last night
cranked out some superweird
sleepmares (you get them night
or day, understand) that I woulda
never believed my skull capable
of containing. Twisted, sick, stark
business. All black and white.
Bella donna bymmers all of them
revolving around a child-molesting
theme. You reckon a man gotta
get himself locked up to free
that kind of crap lodged in the
crannies of his cranium?
   I've put in a request to get
in the kitchen. Get outta this
low rent B Tank do a little
dishwashing, maybe tire myself
into a descent sleep. Also put
in to go before the board that
picks men for the honor camp
that up there so close to the Honda
be almost like going home. Page

DREAMS
SO WIERD
AND FIERCE
That I think for
a while they
ARE PROVOKED
BY THE BROTHER
IN OUR CELL...S

YALE, THEY TELL ME, IS WHERE TO BE IN SWEDEN

first time you know I've
actually lived with spades. And
you know? They are different.

And I spend
A lot of time
thinking about
Heart of Darkness

...Until I watch long
enough and get close
enough to see "different,"
yes, but it's my kind
of difference, and no
provoker of sick
dreams. In fact the
Bloods live healthier under
the gun than any other
group I've encountered.
They've had generations of
practice.
   The dreams go on until
I get my kitchen job...

kind of difference, and no provoker of sick dreams. In fact, the Bloods live healthier lives under the gun than any other group I've encountered. They've had generations of practice.

The dreams go on until I get my kitchen job.

"If they try to pull your covers," Fassenaux feels compelled to advise me, "—retaliate! Pull their motherfucking covers."

His little red-rubber Popeye puss is shoved into my afternoon snakemare. I'm top bunk on a stack of four, so close to the ceiling I bump my head when I sit up too fast.

"Was I talking in my sleep again?"

Instead of answering, Fassenaux launches into one of his tank lessons.

"You know what pulling your covers comes from don'cha? It originates from the old Army barracks shenanigan where you hear a comrade entertaining Mother Thumb and her Four Lovely Daughters. You slip up in the dark and suddenly throw back his blanket to expose him to the ridicule of the rest of the barracks bunkies. Nowdays pulling covers means some dude gets caught in a mistruth. Like our Mr. Szikso over at his mirror f'rinstance. Couple weeks ago he was hitting on me how he's out of smokes could I front him a pack? I say okay what the fuck, but Mr. Cloud the trusty overhears and calls down, 'The lying little bastard got fo' carton in commissary!'—thus pulling the lying little bastard's covers see what I mean?"

"Suck my big member," Szikso says. He's shirtless and sweaty, doing isometrics at the washbasin watching himself flex in the steel mirror. "All those packs went to guards and trusties. Where you think that fresh bar of soap come from? Those fresh towels? From the Felix Szikso Charitable Organization is where."

"Next time you feeling charitable, Mister Felix," Smuthers suggests from the domino table, "get them to issue some fresh armpits." He waves at the air in front of his face, "—because there's some motherfucker in this tank got a funk so powerful it bleachin my 'do!"

All the domino players guffaw and hoot.

"You can all suck my dick," Szikso says, "just as soon as Two-for-two is finished."

Clarence Fassenaux is called Two-for-two Fassen<u>ooo</u> because he managed to stretch a two week sentence to two years for Contempt of Court. Fassenaux ran it down for me when I couldn't sleep my first night.

"Well what it was was I was in traffic court pleading my innocence of some Mickey Mouse infractions, when this nice distinguished fatherly old judge bent down from the bench and says to me: 'Mr. Fastener, while I do not for one instant believe your testimony, I <u>do appreciate</u> your colorful story that you were driving your brother's wife to the maternity ward and I <u>do appreciate</u> your explanation that you lost your license through an insurance error, but I want you to <u>appreciate</u> as well the sanctity of the **LAW** that protects our society. To that end I am going to fine you two hundred dollars or two weeks in the San Mateo County Correctional Facility. Do you appreciate what I'm saying, Mr. Flashinpan?'

"And I says 'Your Honor, what I'm <u>beginning</u> to appreciate is the fact that you are one unfair little <u>turd</u>!' To which he replies, 'Mis-ter Fuzzynose, that will just have to be another two months for Contempt what do you think of that, sir?' To which I sez, 'Your Honor, it strikes me that you are not only a turd you are as well a <u>real asshole</u>!'—and he says 'That will have to be a full year, Mister Fishyfood.' And I says 'Your Honor it is my verdict that you are not only a turd and a asshole, but that you are also one <u>narrowminded mother-fucking little fascist prick</u>!' to which he says 'Two years, take him away,'—and brings the gavel down, WHACK! From that fateful day onward I'm tellin you man I been blood-simple wound-up-tight <u>fearless</u> with these fuckers I don't care what side of the bars they're on!"

Fassenaux's somewhere between 30 and 50, and he slips into a bit of a Creole accent when he's rapping which is most of the time. He had been a Mississippi Delta dockhand most of his life. He said he had come west partly to skip out on some bad debts, and partly to get his little lady and three kids away from the swamps before the skeeters ate 'em up . . . but mainly because he wanted to join Harry Bridge's Longshoremen Union.

"It wasn't just the wages or the benefits, it was Harry. Even as far away as Louisiana the longshoreman scuttlebutts all agreed: Harry Bridges had more basic old-fashioned labor leader <u>balls</u> than those candyass bosses down south! So we come west. A great move. I love San Fran. I was proud to be one of Harry's San Fran Stevedores. Then after a couple years my Little Lady got to missing the mosquitos and moved the kids back to Pontchartrain. Me, I took a room right across the street from the Longshoremen's Hall—a chair, a sack, a crapper and a hotplate. I yam what I yam kyuk kyuk kyuk."

He'd already done eight months tank time when I checked in, so he was brimful of jail-house lore. He took me under his wing, offered advice, explained the fine points on getting special treatment—(got them to front me this ballpoint and this notebook, for instance). When he saw I wasn't sleeping he scammed Cloud to slip me a tin cup of what's referred to as "graveyard stew"—hot milk, molasses, and toast. Worked good. Then when I started having bad dreams it was Popeye-faced cauliflower-eared Two-for-two Fassenaux who listened.

I told him about one particular nightmare. "I used to have it when I was a kid. A huge snake comes hissing up out of a dark hole in the ground, big around as a barrel and God knows how long. You never see the snake's other end—if it has another end. He's just your standard issue symbolic snake, very trite and very Freudian."

"Never mind that," Fassenaux says eagerly. "What's he look like? Where's he come from?"

"Let me see." I close my eyes to recall the dream. "Okay, this last one came up through the asphalt in a Frosty Freeze parking lot just outside of Modesto."

"Modesto? Terrific! Mex'can Cath'lics. Ol' Man Snake got a respectful reception, I hope?"

"Very respectful. People were scrambling in terror for the toilets and phone booths. Women screaming, cars backing into each other. The carhop was this buxom little senorita with roller skates and lotsa eye shadow. She comes skating out with my order and sees the snake and throws her tray at him."

"Good for her." Fassenaux loves the lurid details. His little red-rubber eyelids are snapping shut and open with excitement. "What then? Did he see you?"

"As a matter of fact he did. He shakes off the onion rings and swoops straight to me, practically nose-to-nose. And hey! I just realized: the snake had a face! A nasty, snakey kind of face but it was a face nevertheless. None of my nightmare snakes ever had a face before."

"Whose face? One of our A Tank brothers? They're nasty-faced fuckers each and every one. How about Mister Szikso at the mirror there? He's got nasty on him like flies on a dead possum."

"See this forearm, Fassenaux?" Szikso says, flexing. "I have to get a Deadly Weapons permit to take this arm across the border."

It looks like Don Knotts' arm compared to Popeye's. I check out the other dozen or so in the cell with us and shake my head. "Nope. None of our tank."

"Any scars moles tattoos or other distinguishing marks of identification?"

I tell him I'll go back to sleep and check, and turn over in my bunk. I wake mid afternoon to find everything just like I left it: Szikso is still at the mirror flexing, the domino game is still going, and I've missed lunch. I'm happy to find out Fassenaux has squirrelled me a baloney and Swiss sandwich. Right away he wants a snake report.

"Nope, no marks, scars or tattoos," I tell him. "The face is smooth."

"Smooth? Entirely smooth? Like a baby's plump little cherub-face smooth?"

I nod, marveling I recall the face so well under Fassenaux's prompting. "Like a cherub's."

He snaps his fingers. "Why then, there you are! It's Joe Meeks' face on that snake."

"I haven't ever seen Joe Meeks' face."

"Doesn't matter. What you got, Mister Kesey, is what they call down in the bayous 'tainted sleep.' There's yarbs you can take for it. Next phone call they let me make to my sainted mother I'll have her mail us a bag."

"Yeah sure," Szikso sneers from his spot at the mirror. "And just how you plan to get this bag of yarbs past the mail search, Mister Fassenaux?"

"Oh I got pull, Mister Szikso, I got pull you can't imagine. Maybe I get her to send you along a bar of her lye soap, while I'm at it—see if you can't scrub out some of those things that crawled up in your armpits and died."

"Pull on this, Motherfucker."

"I can pull it if you can find it, Mister Szikso," Fassenaux says sweetly.

The A Tank tenants hoot and laugh. Breems peeks over the top of his blue specs and adds, "Was I you, Mistah Szikso, I wouldn't go one-on-one with Two-for-two mouth-to-mouth! I'm afraid he got you way outgun."

"Fuck you, Breems," is the best retort Szikso can muster, his face reddening.

"See what I mean about covers?" Fassenaux's bringing it all back around to the point he started with hours ago. "Look at poor Mr. Szikso over there blushin—got his covers pulled again!"

"Fuck all of you," Szikso snarls, "and the horse you rode in on."

P.S. kitchen duty may not seem like such a big deal. It only moves you out of the tank about ten paces, to a cramped and steamy food factory down the corridor. A huge black trustey called Cloud rumbles orders at you: "Bring dat pot heah . . . peel dem 'tatos . . . mop up does spill . . ."

If your efforts don't suit Cloud it's "hey gawd put dis lardass back de tank an bring me one ain't scared of wawk."

Even if you do suit him you're still gonna have to put in a week under him rumbling around in the steam before he clears you to walk the line with the serving cart. Then you're out of the tank and out of the kitchen, too! It may not seem like much but that little bit of Out is a big step on the way to some more Out. And after a couple weeks of satisfactory kitchen duty Cloud can recommend you for honor camp consideration. If you pass that interview you get to actually get <u>outside</u>!

Damn this ballpoint is running dry. And they won't le me hav   ther one. Oh well 've got thi   ittle pair f ki dy sci ors an som   mag   s An I can paste st ff down wit th str wbe y jelly th   oods cal red de th. It glu bro en dom nos ba k to eth r don t it?

Dear Faye:

Commissary arrives. A festive event of sugar and shit making you a man of means again. The best deal is a couple of stainless steel blades. When you don't smoke it isn't such a big deal (in fact, it isn't such a big deal for those who do get cigarettes, just a bad deal for them as don't and wisht they <u>did</u>).

Call Ed. Have him contact Duggs concerning those letters of mine that are getting published and have him tell Duggs that the editor has work for me helping if I want it; maybe I can get a work furlough; which puts me out during the day and I come back in at night. See also if there isn't somebody who could get Page an 8-to-5 type job.

All this could mean you and the kids moving back to Palo Alto. Maybe move in with Chloe for a time. You might talk to Duggs yourself and tell him we could use the cash. I told him I'd been working on a farm in Oregon and you and the kids were living in a one-room shack but I don't think he put much stock in it. Everybody assumes I'm either rich or will be rich as soon as I get my next royalty check. Hard to convince folks that the well is dry.

I'm working in the kitchen, on the pushcart, helping a nervous colored dude named Bob. Good guy. Little too good. He don't watch it these boys will choke him like the goose of the golden eggs.

It's a drag in here but I'll survive, maybe even prosper. It's a lot like the VA, only from the other side.

Since I can only get one letter a day, send some mail to Page. He can use it.

Lots of time to think. And listen.

Later   —Ken

Tell the kids I'll write them soon.

BETWEEN BAYSHORE, THE DOG POUND, REDWOOD CITY JAIL AND THE SEWAGE PLANT—

Breezeway—ammonia—waiting for phone chance. My turn comes just at count. After count it's church and "Sorry, dude: the county don't want you making no phone calls during church."

> Song in the library:

> Gettin' short and gettin' horny
> Gettin' tight about gettin' loose
> Doin' hardtime dirty worry
> What's the motherfuckin' use?

Into "You Are My Sunshine," in a key too high: "You lost my mo-ther-fuck-in' ass."

Uncomfortable guitar picking by Vallejo Oakie while we wait for visiting day to open up.

Birthday party in the dusty wind-ripped visiting lot next to Bayshore. Kit, Ed & Family, Paul, Anne & Family plus Chloe plus Paula bring me a cake. The candles won't light in the wind. The sun melts the frosting. We sit with our backs to the barracks in the prime area (with one bench and four tables to 80 prisoners, visiting facilities are at a premium).

We talk of Revelations and which way do we go after the big California quake. Am I a good guy or a bad guy? Finally decide that I must be a good guy because if the guys I oppose are the good guys well fuck it, anyway.

Let me see if I can't color you a little bit, Joe Meeks . . . Joseph Anthony Meeks.

> Will you allow their talk/ to
> trample love's gentle start?
> /Am I after all the beast
> without soul or heart?/A Real
> Dream/the crystal raindrop/
> broke into fragments/crushed
> on window pane./A tear fell /
> bearing sad notes/a melodious
> refrain.

I hear about you from the inmates the day I book in—that you are SMCO Jail's <u>other</u> celebrity: "Joe Meeks . . . the sex fiend you know? Back in the rear cell? . . . He tried to do himself in last night; cut his wrists when he found out they're still shooting for the death penalty the poor motherfucker."

I hear about you from the deputies: "Kesey? Joe Meeks heard you're a author and wanted me to bring you one his poems. Will you read it and maybe write him a note of advice alright?"

"I thought it forbidden, inmates passing notes—?"

"Well . . . in Joe's case—" And left the paper sticking through the bars.

> From the clouds/above the
> raindrop/came into being./From the
> depths/of slumber came/the tear—a
> dream. By Joseph Anthony Meeks.

The only advice I could think to send back was: "Joe. You'll do better writing closer to your veins."—whatever the fuck that means.

As the poems continue to drop by I learn a little more about our sex-fiend poet. "Joe didn't kill anybody leastways the prosecution didn't say so."

> I am awakened,/express the poet
> within/of new poem's fomenting/of
> my enlighten state/poems stand
> unfaltering!

"He pleaded crazy to the charges but got shot down at his sentencing."

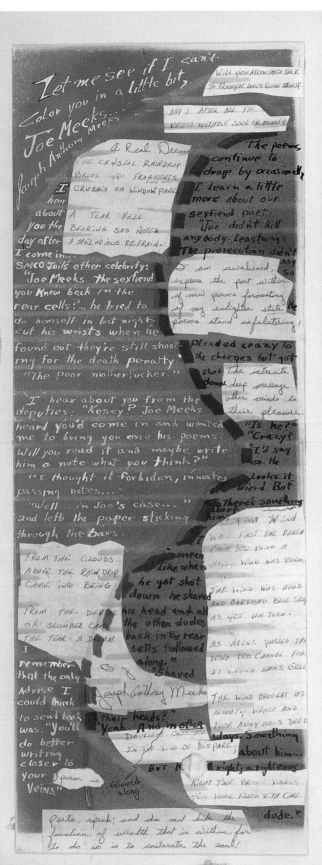
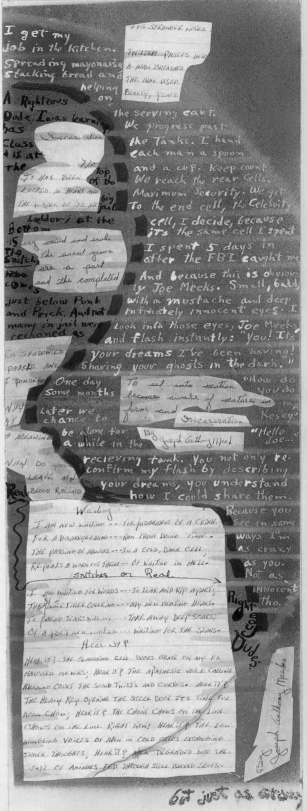

> The intricate/deep message/
> other minds/to their pleasure.

"Is he?" "Crazy?" "Yeah, crazy—" "I'd say so. He looks it. Weird. But there's something about him that <u>gets</u> to you know what I mean? Like when he got shot down he shaved his head and all the other dudes back in the rear cells followed along."

> First wind/ When first the
> earth/came into being a / happy wind
> was born. / The wind was mild/ and
> caressed blue sky/ as yet
> untorn./As aeons passed the/
> wind did change for/it viewed man's
> greed./The wind brought its/ mighty
> wrath and/ took away man's deed.

"Shaved their heads?"

    "Yeah. And <u>other</u> places. Something about him sort of spooky, you know—"

> Daylight finds me/in the void of
> despair;/Nighttime brings visions/
> your voice filled with care.

"—but for a sex fiend he's alright; a righteous dude."

> Poets, speak; and do not hide the/
> fountain of wealth that is within, for/
> to do so is to castrate the soul!/
> It's stronger notes./Twilight passes
> into/a man breathed/the man used/
> Beauty, peace

Then I get my job in the kitchen, spreading mayonnaise and stacking bread and helping with the serving cart. I get to see the rest of the prisoners as we progress past the tanks. Page grins his big toothy grin and gives me a sharp salute, silent, because part of our sentence stipulates we are not to speak to each other for two years.

    I hand each man a spoon and a cup. Keep count. We reach the rear cells. Maximum security. We get to the very last cell and to my surprise it's a cell I'm familiar with. The celebrity-cell, I decide. Because it's the same cell I spent five days in after the FBI caught me on the freeway. Standing meekly behind the bars is obviously Joe Meeks.

He's small, serene and hairless. Not merely bald, but hairless. No whiskers or eyebrows or lashes, skin smooth and pink, eyes blue as a baby boy's booties. I look into those eyes and blurt like a fool, "Fassenaux was right! It is your dream I've been having!"

> To set into motion/become aware of
> nature in/form and incarceration
>   by Joseph Anthony Meeks

"How do you do, Mr. Kesey?"

"Medium rare, Joe," I answer, rattled. "How about you?"

"About the same. But they tell me I'll be well done in another few months."

We share a polite laugh. Gallows humor. Cloud begins negotiating the cart back around, obviously giving us a forbidden chance to talk. Meeks is as serene as I am shook. The only thing I can think of is that chair.

"I stood vigil with Marlon Brando at San Quentin the night before they fried Caryl Chessman. I gave him two Dexedrines."

"Chessman?"

"No. Brando."

"That's nice."

"Yeah he seemed like a nice guy . . ."

"Here's another three poems . . . if it isn't imposing on your time."

"Not at all. I've got all the time in the world."

"That's nice."

I was glad when Mr. Cloud growled it was time to go. After we'd pushed the cart far enough away from Meeks' cell Cloud murmurs, "He some righteous dude."

A righteous dude, I was learning, has class, has a position high up on the jailhouse ladder—

> (incarceration/No/it has been/locked in
> heart and/the whisper of its me.)

—at the bottom of the ladder is the Snitch. The Snitch is ranked even below the Punk and the Prick. At the top is the Righteous Dude, and in between on various rungs are located other castes such as the Mooch and the Sniveler, the Bullshitter, the Brownie and the Boy Scout, also the Backstabber, the Rat and the Standup Con, and on upward to the Righteous Dude . . . and beyond that top rung is the Condemned Man. Makes no difference whether he's innocent or guilty, he is condemned.

> My mind and soul/the uncut gems/are a part/and
> the completed/in shadowed/sparkle and/

I ponder/why/at a meaning/why do you/leave my/
blood racing?

Waiting

I am now waiting . . . for judgement of a crime/
For a disarrayed mind—ran from doing time.
The passing of months—in a cold, dank cell;
Repeats a worn out theme—of waiting in hell.
I am waiting for words—to tear and rip apart;
The inner fiber covering—my now beating heart.
To shed tears will not—take away deep scars;
of a poet now waiting—waiting for the stars.

Hear it?

Hear it? The slamming cell doors grate on my
exhausted nerves; hear it? The apathetic voice calling
morning court the sound twists
            and curves. Hear it?
The heavy key opening the steel door it's time for
noon chow; Hear it? The chant chow's on the line
chow's on the line. Right now! Hear it? The low
mingling voices of men in cold cells exchanging
inner thoughts; hear it? Men degraded into the
state of animals fed through steel barred slots.

by

Joseph Anthony Meeks

Finally after a few weeks I go in for my interview. They want to know: "You ran once, how do we know you won't run again?"

I want to say "You don't." That would be the truth. But I also want out.

"I think my coming to court the other day should indicate I'm ready to do my time."

"Alright, then, Mr. Kesey; what do you think you could do at the camp to help? Assuming you go, that is."

"The same thing I always do."

"And that is?"

—the wrong answer from his tone. So I add "The same uh . . . talking with people . . . try to point out uh . . . blind spots and help—"

"Mr. Kesey, there may be drugs at the camp; what would you do if offered some pot?"

"Turn it down."

"And?"

"That's all. I don't plan to turn anybody in."

"This is an honor camp, Mr. Kesey; would we have your word that you would abide by all its rules?"

"Of course."

THEY SAY <u>YES</u>. Two hours later I'm on my way to the redwoods.

So sudden you ask? Holy <u>Mother</u> sudden I tell you! One minute we're moping around A Tank looking down the barrel of another long dark potentially explosive weekend, the next minute Deputy Rhack is at the bars hollering "half dozen lucky bastards for honor camp line up in the order I call your name: Szikso, Felix; Smuthers, Jefferson; Breems, A. C.; Kesey, Ken; Fassenaux, Clarence. String 'em up, Mr. Cloud . . ."

We follow Rhack down a courthouse corridor, five of us linked together shacklefile along 20 foot of heavy chain. Szikso first, close up behind Rhack as befits his brown-nosey rank; then Smuthers, wearing a floppy knit cap of many colors; then Breems, wagging his blueshaded head side to side like he was listening to Little Stevie Wonder on a private frequency; then me; then Fassenaux, carrying a wad of extra chain. We make a stop by the infirmary and pick up the sixth of our half-dozen . . . a mysterious black stranger none of us has ever clapped eyes on until Deputy Rhack leads him out of the infirmary.

"You're in luck, campers. You got a new playmate. Say hello to Silver Willy."

We're dumbstruck by the ponderous sight of this man, even the loquacious Fassenaux—hell, even Smuthers and Breems, and they're participants in the same race! Because I mean to tell you this is one double-bad looking . . . ah, looking . . . (what the hell do I call them? Think of the thousand names hung on them trailing back into the darkest alleys of our racist past: coon; jig; darky; shine; Sambo; Jim Crow; buck; spearchucker etc etc. I always kinda fancied the hepcat name, Spades, until the time Roland Kirk and his group dropped by La Honda for a ceremonial visit, and I called somebody a spade. Jerry Garcia called me aside to whisper "Hey, Keez . . . the appelation 'spade' is permissible only if you're a jazz musician."

I tried the formal name, Negroes, until M'kehla informed me that They would rather be called "Afro American expatriots." By the time I could say this without stuttering, "Afro Americans" was out and "Blacks" was in— unless you were behind bars with them in which case "Bloods" was allowed. But this guy isn't exactly Blood, and he damn sure isn't black. Black don't even come close. This guy is midnight purple!)

—anyway, one very bad looking guy. And as we're soon to learn, that's his <u>good</u> side.

We mumble various greetings but he doesn't turn our way. He's not very tall—just about eye-level to Rhack's Adam's apple while he gets one of his cuffs unlocked. And he probably doesn't weigh much more than me if we're just talking pounds. But he's too heavy to measure in pounds. He's like a black hole, a <u>purple</u> black hole, sucking in light like a blotter. Rhack links him to the end of our chain and gives a good yank to be sure it's secure.

The man doesn't budge. He just stands there, massive as an anchor. "Mau mau," Breems breathes, barely hearable.

"All set, campers?" Rhack heads back to the front of our little file, wiping his hands on his brown necktie. Our new playmate does a slow left face our direction—just enough to give us a glimpse of his other side before we're tugged back around lockstep. He has an appalling scar across his face, nearly an inch wide and ten inches long, slicing from his hairline clear down to the opposite collarbone, right across the eye socket, leaving the eyeball a smoldering sulphurous yellow.

You could feel that smolder right through the chain.

Deputy Rhack already had a seating arrangement in mind. A big panting police dog was riding shotgun thank you very much. Next to him was Szikso, sharing the middle seat with a .270 deer rifle. Fassenaux was assigned the right side of the pickup's stingy back seat—"I want as much distance from you as I can get, Motormouth," Rhack explained. "Then Breems then Smuthers. Kesey? You and Prisoner Sylvester are the biggest; you get to ride in the truckbed with the laundry and mail. Sun will do you both good. Sit backwards and give me the chain."

He threaded it through our cuffs, then around the spare tire. "You can drag some those mailbags to you for cushions. I gave you plenty of slack."

As the pickup pulled away from the courthouse, Prisoner Sylvester looked at the piles of excess chain spilling out of his lap like tarnished intestines, and spoke his first word:

"Slack."

Then he pulled a pair of old time airplane goggles out of his pocket and strapped them on and wadded up his handkerchief, which he pressed against his nose and mouth. He didn't mutter another sound until an hour or so later, up near Skylonda.

We took an unscheduled detour off 84 and bumped our way down a rutted road to a little trailer house snuggled back in the junipers.

The scene looked both temporary and dug in at the same time. There were no electric wires, no water main. Empty bottles shimmered in sunny collections everywhere. Red geraniums had been lined up to indicate a path, but they weren't in pots. They had been carefully planted in Ripple bottles. A clothesline flapped a gay display of Hawaiian muu-muus and lacy undergarments. A big greasy Harley was chained to the clothesline pole like a bad dog.

Deputy Rhack hopped out, grinning like a cat that hadn't eaten the canary yet, but knew there was one on the menu.

"This is my biker brother's spread. He's in traction. I told him I would check in on his old lady from time to time."

He told the four guys wedged in the rig to leave the motor idling so the air conditioner would work.

"And how's our outdoor campers back here in the rear?"

"Dry," Silver told him through the hankie. I hadn't been sure he was conscious.

"Why of course you are, Mr. Sylvester. Let me fill one of these bottles for you. How about you, Mister Kesey? You want to wet your whistle? I can rinse out another Ripple bottle . . . ?"

I told him I'd share with prisoner Silver. "But I could use some sun lotion. Can I have my personals box?"

"Well of course you can," Rhack bubbled, beaming with goodfellowship. When he located my box he generously handed over the lotion and let me have this pen and this notebook in the bargain.

"All of you behave yourself. Just sit tight and leave the air conditioner running and keep the windows shut. This won't take but a shake of the lamb's tail."

Fassenaux had the rear window slid open before Rhack was two steps away.

"So that's what the dapper deputy-about-town calls it these days: a lamb's tail. That's simply too too-too. Ain't that just simply too-too, Mr. Mau Mau Breems?"

"Mau too mau," Breems agrees, watching Rhack stride off down the path. "But I got to tell you, I am shocked. I thought this big old rifle was all the sexual relation Deputy Gun Rhack needed. I am deeply shocked."

Fassenaux kyuk kyuks his Popeye chuckle. "That's how come he didn't take the rifle with him—so it wouldn't know he's two-timin."

SMUTHERS: "I can't fuckin believe he left it here with us criminals."

SZIKSO: "I got an idea. Let's take that gun and shoot this shiteatin dog and take this vehicle and make our escape."

FASSENAUX: "Good plan, Mister Szikso. You're closest to the gun, the dog, and the steerin wheel, you do it. I want to see whether you're a chickenshit or a fool."

Before Szikso can answer I hear an ominous murmur from my left. "It's a setup."

"Which is it, Mister Szikso? Chickenshit or fool?"

"Fassenoo, you don't have the brains to tell one from another."

"Well then we could take a vote, Mister Szikso, from partymembers present—"

"I've heard about those Longshoreman's votes, Fassenaux. I heard they're held under what they call The Big Red Bridge."

"Now you've done it, Szikso! Insulting Harry Bridges? You've shown your true colors. You are a company goon!"

"Moon goon," Breems says, bobbing his head. Smuthers commences whistling an abstract jazz accompaniment. The dog pants rhythm. Szikso and Fassenaux chime in like dueling saxophones, honking back and forth in the key of Harry Bridges.

Once more, from my left, like the deepest note on a double bass: "It's a setup."

That was exactly twenty-six minutes ago. I know because I finally get my wristwatch out of my personals box and get it cleaned up enough to tell the time. All the stuff in my box is covered with white powder—my shaving stuff and my toothbrush and toothpaste and my

Coppertone and my wallet pictures (no wallet or credit cards or ID, tho). It's the cornstarch Faye had insisted I pack in case of jock itch. The familiar Argo Cornmaiden box had been sliced wide open and the white powder spread all through everything, including this note-book.

Sylvester speaks again, loud. "I don't like it."

"You mean all this powder? It's just cornstarch."

"I mean this whole setup— that rifle; that keyring left in the ignition; pickup still running . . ."

Smuthers stops whistling and says he can fix that still-running part. He reaches over the front seat for the ignition and Grr**rrOOF!**—the dog makes a vicious lunge and Smuthers barely gets away with his hand. "Mother<u>fuck</u>!" The dog commences barking and snarling like a Mississippi bloodhound. This brings Rhack peeking out the screen door, the sister-in-law in orange bathrobe peeking over his shoulder.

"Fuck Jesus," Szikso exclaims, twisting away from the windshield. "I know that bitch. She thinks I hung a bunch of bad paper on her down in San Jose two years ago. I <u>knew</u> there was something about that stuff on the clothesline." He twists the other direction. "Smuthers, I need a disguise. Let me have that goddam cap!" As he reaches back the dog lunges barking at <u>him</u>.

The spectacle gives our dapper deputy and the sister-in-law a good laugh, and they duck back in the trailer. The screen door whacks shut and the woman appears behind it, leisurely trading the bathrobe for a muu-muu as though the screen made her invisible. "You see <u>that</u>?" I ask my traveling companion.

"I don' hardly see jack outta that side anymore— and that's my good side."

I'm relieved to find out he has one.

"What that book?"

"My journal? I draw and write shit in it. You want to see?" I hold it out to him and he lifts the goggles and takes a jaundiced look—one eye sulphurous, the other hepatitis.

He hands back the book and lowers the antique goggles. They're so silly looking he feels he has to explain.

"They in case I go someplace where I need them, to keep out dust and shit blowin around—like in backa The Man's pickup."

—a voice so heavy it's beyond sardonic or bitter or cynical. It groans under a burden of sorrow so immense it sounds Biblical.

Rhack comes loping back out, canary feathers sticking out of his bird-eating grin. He slides beneath the wheel and pops the gear into reverse.

"Next stop, bunkies, Camp Pom**poONIO**oo!"

Now it's The Man's turn to whistle, all the way over Skyline, Battle Hymn of the Republic, his eyes has seen the GLORY. The only time his whistling ceases is when we see a deer grazing in the roadside weeds. "Pissfire, it's a doe"—and goes back to his whistling.

First look at Camp. Incredible wholesome scene, neat and practical . . . wasn't for the cop uniforms you'd think it was a Boy Scout camp. Fassenaux is the first to put a cap on the look of it.

"Hey Deputy Rhack, who was it you said was captain of this camp?"

"Walter Trueheart. Captain Walter Trueheart."

"Oh. I thought maybe you said Walter Disney."

A dozen or so prisoners are fiddling around in the chickpeas in front of the office. They check us out from beneath sweated brows—especially Sylvester and me. They got on lowtop workboots, gloves, and matching blue denim pants and shirt. No numbers. They scope us over good as we pull in, weeding and trimming while Rhack circles slow around them. The chickpeas have been arranged to spell H O N O R, with flagpoles coming out the middle of each O. One pole sports a fresh stars-and-stripes; the other the California Grizzly Bear.

Rhack rolls to a stop at the bottom of a wide flight of split-log steps leading up to a shaded front porch. "You men wait here." A noisy scrub jay on the porch rail announces our arrival as Rhack goes bounding up the steps two at a time. This time he takes the rifle with him.

"The clip was up under the dash," Szikso whispers. "I caught him checking for it when we seen that doe."

"By gosh Mister Szikso, yer smarter'n you look."

"He'd of shot her, too, if that PG&E truck hadn't happened by."

Rhack returns and lets the men out of their cramped seating. Fassenaux goes prancing around kicking up the rich dirt like some kind of farmer clown. "Soil! First I've seen in eight months. I'm ecstatic!"

"Fool gonna see static," Sylvester murmurs, "if he don't stop stirrin up that dust."

Rhack unchains me and Sylvester and we climb out. "Captain Trueheart is up at the Speckles mansion, raising money. You gents are going to be oriented by Sergeant Wayne."

Fassenaux is still prancing around. "Zip a dee dew daw zip dee hey you field hands! Is it always this nice? Hey Deputy Rhack cheer up, it's a lovely day!"

"Fassenaux, I don't know but what I should drive you back to the tank. You might be just too loose to be loose. Here! Some of you landscrapers . . . give me a hand carrying these bags to Commissary."

The landscrapers that rush to carry the bags are all black. They want a closer look at this bad motherfucker Brother. Sylvester stands unmoving under their gaze, his scar shining like jewelry in the slanting sun. As they scope him over you can almost hear the secret clicking of priorities being shifted around.

"Happenin' Bro?" one of the braver landscrapers asks politely, trying to draw him out.

"Ain't jack happenin'," Sylvester rumbles, refusing to be drawn out by anybody, bro or no.

"Attention you new campers. Here's your personals." Rhack hands out the boxes as he reads the names. "No, don't open 'em. You have to turn them over to the sergeant for inspection first. Now, up those steps, through the mess hall, and knock at the camp office.

You'll recognize it by the words written on the door—'Camp Pomponio Office'—unless you can't read. Anybody can't read? Good. Okay, pay attention; this is gonna be your Official Admissions Briefing.

"And a word of advice: John Wayne is the head honcho of this ranch, and John sets great store in good first impressions."

"John <u>Wayne</u>?" Smuthers wants to make sure he heard right.

"That's right, Pilgrim," Rhack grins. "John Wayne. Now wagons <u>ho</u>!"

Sylvester ambles next to me as we cross the mess hall. "Give me that book," he says. I ask why and he repeats the command. "Give me the motherfucking book. They won't be checking my box for books. They know I can't read."

The door of the office had been hand-hewn from a solid slab of redwood. The name Camp Pomponio Office wasn't written on the door, it was carved—and I don't mean carved <u>into</u> the wood. The letters were raised, at least half an inch. It was the rest of the redwood that had been cut away. Szikso ran his fingers over the polished letters with obscene zest.

"Tell me this didn't cost some miserable motherfucker about ten months."

Smuthers nods, "I can dig it."

"Don't dig it 'til you've knocked it," Fassenaux quips and gives the redwood three light raps.

"Who is it?"

We looked at each other. "Why it's just <u>us</u>, Cap'n!" Fassenaux informed the voice.

"Goddamn you, Fassenaux," Szikso hissed. "So much for good first impressions. No wonder they didn't approve your camp request eight times. <u>It's six new men from Redwood</u>," he says to the door. "<u>Deputy Rhack told us to knock</u>."

"Well come on in."

You knew the man before you saw him. It was the familiar baritone of John Wayne, a lugubrious voice—weighed down with world-weary resignation and disillusion result of lotsa experience dealing with spineless lowlife backstabbing disappointments just like us. We shuffle in and the big door closes by its own weight. The desktop is a single slab of redwood as well.

The man was looking out an open window, his back to us. He was watching two young prisoners, one white and one black, trying to push a big lawnroller up a lumpy slope. The roller was a 50-gallon drum, leaking around the axle. The two kids were having a terrible time. The roller kept veering off one way then the other, and the slope was slick with water. The sergeant shook his head, chuckling.

"I've been watching for nearly a half hour. I got a little wager going, see, between my Optimistic Angel and my Pessimistic Devil: will these sturdy lads figure out that it's labor-saving easier to pull a load up a hill than it is to push it?" He shook his head in a burlesque show of woe. "Well, shucks. It appears to me the angel is going to lose once again. Oh, I

<u>could</u> holler these labor-saving hints out to them, I know, but I won't. You want to know why I won't? It's because I am comforted by the conclusion that stupidity is its own reward. Who am I to deprive those poor nitwits of their reward?"

This comforted him so much he said it again: "Stupidity . . . is its own reward." Then he turned around and said it a third time, to make sure all of us got it. "Wouldn't you have to agree, gentlemen? Yesterday my angel and my devil were betting whether those same boys would figure out that it would make more sense to haul it to the top of the hill empty <u>then</u> fill it with water, instead of filling it down at the tool shed and having to sweat it up a three-degree grade. You'd think they could figure that out, wouldn't you? Well, wouldn't you?"

It was like him asking "Who is it?" when we knocked. He damn well knew who it was. And we knew that he wasn't after an answer—he was just baiting us. But Fassenaux was not the sort to let many questions go unanswered, baited or no.

"I would say it would depend on whether they were trying to save time or sweat, Cap'n."

"You would would you, Mister Fassenaux?" he asked with his mocking chuckle. "But why would they be interested in saving time? Why would any of you jokers care about saving time? Time is what you got a excess of. You got time up the gump stump. You got time to spend, time to lend; time to taste, time to waste. If you didn't have time to waste you would not <u>be</u> here would you now? You all <u>know</u> you're here because you broke a couple of pissant laws. If you were real stand-up criminals you would be up in San Quentin pulling serious <u>man</u> time, instead of out here in the boonies at Camp Mickey Mouse."

We fidgeted and shuffled. It was a cold shot, aimed at all of us, but oddly it was not fired in any kind of self-righteous or malicious way. It was more the way old drinkin' buddies rag on each other.

His tirade over, he sighed languidly and lowered himself into an old wooden swivel chair. He crossed his boots on the desk and leaned back, hands behind his head. His hair was grizzled gray and curly. His face was creased and gullied by years of booze and sun, then smoke-cured with squinting into campfires. Steely blue eyes twinkled through the squint. Yup; except for that wry twinkle of mischief, it was Ol' Duke Wayne all the way.

"Okay let's get down to business. First off, gentlemen, I will give you my philosophical outlook, so there will be no mistake as to where I stand. From its very inception three years ago I believed this playground to be a damned bleeding-hearts stupid fucking idea. I believed so then, I believe so now, and I shall continue to believe so even if we rehabilitate your worthless asses every one. Because sweat is <u>always</u> the issue, Mister Fassenaux, not time. Wouldn't you all agree? That sweat is always the main issue?"

His blue eyes snapped from face to face to make sure his philosophical outlook had found its targets, then went on.

"This is how it is. That lovely handcrafted nameplate you see before you on this darling redwood desk may say Captain Walter Trueheart but the head honcho at this camp is yours very truly, Sergeant Johnathan Wayne and not one! fucking! wisecrack! you hear what I'm saying? <u>Sergeant</u> Johnathan Wayne, and I run this cute little camp. Captain Trueheart is simply too busy. He's got to be off tending his trapline, to bag enough bleeding hearts to pay for this playground's upkeep. He drops by once or twice a month with a gaggle of supporters and reporters and gives them the tour, flips through the roster, picks up his mail . . . and that's pretty much it. He tells me to keep up the good work, slaps me on the back and he is outta here. I'm what they call the Real Ramrod, The Man, the Big Cheese, the Whole Enchilada! You give me bullshit I'll give you back horseshit. You give me the straight I might just <u>might</u> give you the straight back."

He sat up and bent down to our rapsheets on his desk. Fassenaux caught my eye. Thinking himself shielded by a letter basket, he pursed his lips and gave me the jack-off gesture. I agreed with a slight nod.

"Fassenaux, Clarence!" the sergeant bellowed. "Two-for-two yap-bigger-than-his-brain Clarence Fassenoo no don't you <u>dare</u> say it! I'll rip days faster than that judge at your traffic court."

He slapped Fassenaux's sheet down and picked up another.

"Sylvester, William! 'A walking timebomb' what it says here . . . got a button bigger than his ass or his brain. Let me have a look at you, Silver Willy. Yep I can see it. It's got a little sign under it: 'PUSH BUTTON HERE.' What are the monumental odds of your holding your mud, Mr. Timebomb? Mixed in with redneck bikers from Oakland and bigots from Texas? And take those fucking goggles off! This ain't some World War One airfield."

Sylvester removed the goggles. Wayne's steely-eyed squint went wide for a second at the sight. He covered his shock by bending back over the rapsheets.

"Breems, A. C.! What's A. C. stand for, Mr. Breems? Acid and Cocaine?"

"It changes, your honor."

"Changes? Well okay what's it stand for this month?"

"Always Cool."

"Jay-zus! And you were allowed to wear those cute little specs down in Redwood?"

"They perscription."

"Lawd hab mussy. Are you associated with this flower child, Mr. Sylvester?"

"By circumstances," Sylvester answers.

"Then put your damned goggles back on. I don't want some *Sunset Magazine* subscriber to think I'm playing favorites."

Shaking his head he bent back to the sheets.

"Smuthers, Jefferson. Hasn't paid child support in twenty months. Alimony neither. Well you are going to be in good company here, Mr. Smuthers. More than half of our student body enjoy similar beefs."

"They ain't my kids."

"So fucking what? You probably got plenty of yours being paid for by some other miserable motherfucker . . . Szikso, Felix!"

Szikso snapped to rigid attention. "That's me, Captain."

"A paper-hanging punk, doesn't have nuts enough to knock over a 7-11 or roll a lush.

My, my, my, just look at this list. Sounds like you got your art hung in banks from San Diego to Chico. But such pissant amounts! Two bucks . . . five bucks and seventy-five cents. Jesus, here's a beauty! Last July you bounced a seven dollar check off a wetback paperboy in Chula Vista! Have you no pride?"

"I have my own pride, Captain."

"What can you find to be proud of? More bounce to the ounce? More grunt to the runt?"

When he laughed you couldn't help but join in. He leaned back and crossed his boots on the table again. He clacked the bootsoles together and turned his gaze my direction.

"And that brings us to our celebrity, Mr. Kesey, Ken. You gentlemen appreciate who you're going to be spending time with? 'The West Coast's most promising author' *Time* magazine called him. Herb Caen wonders if he might be 'ring leader of a psycho-deltic cult.' My personal favorite was the jacket Judge John Di Mateus hung on him in court. Maximum John called him 'a tarnished Galahad.'"

He skimmed through the rapsheet shaking his head. He finally tossed it back on the desk. "The truth is I'm too briefed-out to give you the attention you deserve, Mr. Kesey. We'll take a rain check if that's alright with you?"

"Quite all right, Captain."

"We'll enjoy a bit of a *tattoo tate* sometime later on down the well-known line, do you follow me?"

"Only out of morbid curiosity," I almost say, but nod instead.

"Then follow that yellow line to supply and draw yourself some boots and gloves. You stout lads are going to hoe weeds in the ice plants out front. All rookies hoe the ice plants for a week, whether they need it or not. Get your hoes from those other hoe-ers. They can show you what's a weed and what isn't. Tell them they are dismissed for the rest of the day—"

"Excuse me, Captain," Breems interrupted, holding up his hand like a schoolboy. "I be cool but not too stout." He pulled up a pant leg to reveal a misshapen ankle. "Can you dig it?"

Wayne shuddered. "Godamighty cover it back up! Gentlemen, that repulsive sight we just seen is an example of one of the side effects of LSD. Alright Mr. Breems; you draw a trowel instead of a shovel. Cool, crippled or stupid, everybody works in the yard their first week, just so I can keep my eye on them. Can you dig <u>that</u>, Mr. Breems?"

"Hey if he can't dig it," Fassenaux pipes up in his Popeye voice, "he can <u>trowel</u> it."

"Oh you are a mixer aren't you, Fassenaux? He's a mixer isn't he, gentlemen? Now all of you—get your stupid mugs out of my sight . . . and stop calling me captain!"

Back out in the mess hall Fassenaux says, "That part about stupidity being its own reward? I could get behind that."

After we've switched places with the landscrapers, the sergeant comes out with a cold Coke and takes a seat in a porch swing. He sips and watches and grins, the bastard. On the other hand it's absolutely great to be out in the sun, scratching at the overworked earth, sweating out the poisons built up by three weeks in the Redwood City tanks. Everybody's happy to be hoe hoe hoeing even if it's only makework work. Except after twenty minutes or so, Sylvester goes to sneezing and wheezing, and big yellow tears start draining out of his goggles. I ask him if he's okay.

"Hush," he whispers. "It just allergies, they go away in a bit. Don't let on."

But it's too late. Wayne's already noticed. He gets up from the porch swing, shading his eyes our direction.

"Sylvester? Step back into my office if you would . . ."

A few minutes later the big gloomy man is shackled and loaded back into the rear of Rhack's pickup. Fassenaux's at my side, watching the pickup pull away.

"See what's happening, Mr. Kesey? The poor motherfucker needs hay fever medicine so they're trucking his ass back down to Redwood, back in the <u>back</u> of the pickup! Is that cold or what?"

CAMP POMPONIO

—Suddenly from guards and cells to walking unguarded through <u>TREES</u> and <u>TIME</u> only a half a dozen miles or so from the place we were busted.

BARRACKS . . . "A" stood, it seemed, for Age. Lots of old dudes doing time behind drunks. One of the best naps I've ever napped was in A Barracks. "B" I found later stood for Bad. B Barracks seldom ate first. And "C" stood for Kook.

ICE PLANTS. "All right, all you new men work in the ice plants until you get a real job assignment. Clip the spots where it's thick and plant the clippings in the spots where it's thin. Check you out a shovel or a pick or something."

Meaning: look busy!

MESS HALL, where they feed us. Also where Big Group is held twice weekly—heavy vibrationszzz.

OFF LIMITS: WOODS . . . too many possibilities in the brush for hanky-panky. Except for county park work; Monday-thru-Friday the men working outside of camp ride out at 8:30 AM in the back of a county works dumptruck, bounce and grind for 45 minutes to dig ditches or chop weeds . . . then return at four.

OFFICERS' QUARTERS: the deputies are on three days then off three.

SEWAGE PLANT that whines night and day in a high, subtle and irritating E-sharp.

TAILOR SHOP: soon to erupt as the hot spot its reputation boasted it to be.

RHACK'S GARDEN: fresh lettuce, radishes and tomatoes that'll cost you five days if you're caught stealing.

BALL FIELD: any ball hits a branch it's out of play.

Camp Days

TUESDAY AFTERNOON

Getting to know the place and the people, the routine and the ritual.

Ain't no bad life . . . three good meals a day, good bed, nice little office of my own in my tailor shop—

"Daisy, Daisy . . . " strums into the redwoods.

A deputy putts down the hill on his Honda.

We got plenty clubs and activities and interests . . . like a health spa with cops.

Something (what could it be?) sends the deputy searching . . . Got your own private locker that you can keep your zu-zu's in, and nobody can get in except the deputies. Nothing the matter with a setup like that, right?

Getting to know the place and the people. The routine and the ritual. **TUESDAY AFTERNOON**

Ain't no bad life... 3 good meals a day, good bed, nice little office of my own — my tailor shop—

Daisy, Daisy... strums into the redwoods. A deputy putts down the hill on his Honda 17.

I'm going through the commissary line. Names being called alphabetically.

THUR. MORN.

"Who handin' out the Zu-zus?"
"Dep'tee Grainger."
"He back, huh?"
"Yeah. The motherfucker."

Grainger is behind the counter, surrounded by cartons of cigarettes and candy. He's tan, alert and ornery looking. Mean talking but there's a humor under the growl. Old big-hearted sarge.

"So you're Kesey." Glowers. He has a few opinions on current trends in the younger generation and don't care if those opinions show.

I tell him, yeah, I'm Kesey and give him a big friendly grin in return for his glowers. He

2
spots my tooth. "Gimme that tooth again," he orders. Tips his head and squints into my mouth.

"Jee-zus Kee-rist!" He turns to the deputy helping him with commissary. "You see that?" The other deputy nods and they both give it the Jack Webb bit of "Aint things in a shit of a shape?"

And I pick up my bag of goodies to leave but Grainger stops me, that glower's like a 3rd degree interogation lamp.

"What'd you come back for?" he asks. Straight. Meaning from Mexico. Where I had it safe and groovy. Lots of cops want to know this. I got various answers according to the ego-needs of the man. Sometimes I answer funny, sometimes deep esoteric phylisophical, sometimes nationalistic ("I'de rather be in jail in America than free in Mexico.") sometimes religious as with Wright. The right answer in Grainger's case is obviously the Stars and Stripes — he wouldn't quite believe it but he's John Wayne enough to want to.

But I can't pull it off quite. Grainger reminds me too much of my Dad. His stance too beligerant. So I give him my grimmest and dead levelest look and tell him:

SATURDAY

3
"Because I wasn't finished."

Click! Our eyes hold. I can feel him probe for clues to my seriousness. I can tell he knows what I'm talking about just about as clearly as I do, but doesn't know whether to buy it. Decides to withhold judgement. Click. Big twinkling smile. Then calls out the next name on the commissary list. Whew!!!!!

A very fierce dude, Grainger. Been a cop long time and aint about to stand for any shit. And none of the usual cop paranoia about him to make him hesitate. We get commissary once a week if you got cash on the books... pens, paper, candy bars and razor blads.

I think I like him.
I know he scares me.
Oh well, I got my Zu-zu's
Cigarettes if you smoke...

plenty of clubs and activities and interests

Like a Health Spa with cops---

We got clubs and activities and interests

your own private locker that you can keep your Zu-zus in and nobody can get in except the deputies.

Nothing the matter with a set-up like that right?

you got a band comes up and plays for you, whether you want to Listen OR NOT

Also on the 3rd saturday afternoon each month

FRI
Gravel & but

We are the cream of San Mateo criminals... an experiment in positive punishment. very nice very nice.

I'm called into the office shortly after what I feel is a pretty fair meeting, vibration wise to tell with the Crossfield (he never made contact)

SAT: 1:15 Entertainment COUNTY compulsory! ...be there

"When whatever I Call" (you better fuckin' answer friend.)

One of the docs ambles by onto high ground, punching his ball mitt. "Hows the atmosphere down there?" "Oh I've felt better and, and I've felt worse." "Can you dig it." "I can dig it." Well let's see now. I'd like my wife + kids but if that's impossible I'll settle for some SOUND and some DOPE!

THURSDAY MORNING

I'm going through the commissary line. Names being called alphabetically.

"Who handin' out the zu-zu's?"

"Deputy Wayne."

"He back, huh?"

"Yeah. The motherfucker."

Wayne is behind the counter, surrounded by cartons of cigarettes and candy. He's tan, alert, and ornery looking. Mean talking, but there's humor under the growl. Old big-hearted sarge.

"And here's our Mr. Kesey." Glowers. He has a few opinions on current trends in the younger generation and don't care if those opinions show.

I give him a big friendly grin in return for his glower. He spots my American flag tooth. "Gimme that tooth again," he orders. Tips his head and squints into my mouth.

"Jee-zus Kee-rist!" He turns to the deputy helping him with commissary. "You see that?" The other deputy nods and they both give it the Jack Webb bit of "Ain't things in a shit of a shape?" And I pick up my bag of goodies to leave but Wayne stops me; that glower's like a third degree interrogation lamp.

"What'd you come back for?" he asks. Straight. Meaning from Mexico. Where I had it safe and groovy. Lots of cops want to know this. I've got various answers according to the ego-needs of the man. Sometimes I answer funny, sometimes deep esoteric philosophical, sometimes nationalistic ("I'd rather be in jail in America than free in Mexico"), sometimes religious. The right answer in this case is obviously the Stars and Stripes—he wouldn't quite believe it, but he's John Wayne enough to want to.

But I can't pull it off quite. Wayne reminds me too much of my dad. His stance is too belligerent. So I give him my grimmest and dead levelest look and tell him: "Because I wasn't finished."

Click! Our eyes hold. I can feel him probe for clues to my seriousness. I can tell he knows what I'm talking about just about as clearly as I do, but doesn't know whether to buy it. Decides to withhold judgement. Click. Big twinkling smile. Then calls out the next name on the commissary list. Whew!!!!!!!

A very fierce dude, Wayne. Been a cop long time and ain't about to stand for any shit. And none of the usual cop paranoia about him to make him hesitate.

I think I like him.

I know he scares me.

Oh well, got my zu-zu's.

We get commissary once a week if you got cash on the books . . . Pens, paper, candy bars and razor blades. Cigarettes, if you smoke . . .

FRIDAY: GROVEL CLUB

At Group Meeting, Vincent blows it. Buckner gets up to point out parliamentary procedure. Here's the crux—need to take a look at basic training in toastmastering. Then an hour about rules.

A pretty fair meeting, vibration-wise.

SATURDAY: 1:15

On the third Saturday afternoon each month you got a band comes up and plays for you whether you want to listen or not.

Entertainment COUNT! Compulsory! <u>BE THERE!</u>

When whippoorwills CALL (you better fuckin' answer, friend).

MOON RIVER . . .

One of the Bloods ambles by on the high ground, punching his ball mitt. "How's the atmosphere down there?"

"Oh, I've felt better, and I've felt worse."

"Can you dig it?"

"I can dig it."

We are the cream of San Mateo criminals . . . an experiment in positive punishment. Very nice, very nice. Only one or two changes I might make.

My attorney asks "What would you like up here?"

Huh? Well letsee now. I'd like my wife and kids but if that's impossible I'd settle for some SOUND and some COLOR and some DOPE.

"Come on in," says Fassenaux at the
urinal . . . "Watch my organ recital."

C BARRACKS—HOME

By the way . . .
HAVE YOU SEEN
THE GREAT
WHITE
DUCK?

C Barracks is a long clean chicken house sort of Quonset hut, divided in the middle by the dayroom and the head. The chicken roosts are neatly made single bunks spaced by neat gray metal lockers on the neat off-white tile floor. More a ward than a barracks. Inspection every day at 1:30 during which time such barracks are emptied except the inspecting deputy and the housemother scoping through with a score sheet on a clipboard . . . Inspector calls out blackmarks, housemother writes them down. Barracks with least amount of blackmarks at week's end gets to the line first for chow the following week.

"Who got first today?" This is Vincent, a 300-pound wad of leavened dough white as flour.

"Who gives a shit?"

"No, I mean really. We're tied right now with B Barracks for Christ sake. You want to be eatin after <u>them</u> bad motherfuckers?"

B Barracks is Bad and they know it. Trail the rapist is in B. Plus Henry the Samoan bar brawler plus Bostic the pimp with cleaver scars. "Should see the <u>other</u> motherfucker." Bad dudes all and none of B Barracks expect to eat first. Nevertheless the deputies make sure grades stay pretty close right up to Saturday when they have the <u>Big Inspection</u>, tally the score and announce first, second and third in the chow line for the following week.

"I mean, who really <u>gives</u> a shit just as long as we eat?"

"Well keep in mind that them that go first get first at seconds." This is The Gimp, a dedicated crystal geezer looks like a dried fish with a dirty cast on one hind flipper.

"Do <u>you</u> eat seconds, motherfucker?"

"Sometimes."

"Bullshit. I never saw you go for seconds but for pork chops."

"And cake."

"Bullshit; you get plenty to eat up here <u>whenever</u> you eat. I ain't gonna bust my ass tryin' to get top score in being neat."

C Barracks generally eats first just the same. Strange, too, considering our housemother is a tubby jazz bass player neurotic speed freak named Welah, pulling hard time behind writing script, like The Gimp. An old time street shooter who remembers when you could buy methedrine in "jugs" for a dollar a box. Spends a lot of his time sitting cross-legged on his bunk reading history books or playing hearts, putting off his housemotherly duties until the men have to pitch in and help out in exasperation at the last moment.

"Shit-all-mighty, Welah. You ain't done <u>nothin</u>!"

"Not a motherfuckin <u>thing</u> and it ain't ten minutes before inspection."

"Gentlemen. Please. Just shut the fuck up and lend a hand in our moment of need."

We bustle around until the call "Here comes the man!" Everybody's stashing last-minute dust rags and sponges and going through their bunks and Welah walking round-eyed and sweating and fidgety beside the deputy checking the cobwebs in the heater and dust on the top of the fire extinguisher.

SUNDAY, VISITING DAY

Ed McClanahan brings me up some notebooks and pens, plus Gordon comes to visit. He's turned away, not being on my list, but as he leaves he gives a small bottle of yellow paint to the dude working the parking lot. After visiting is over, this dude tells me of the transaction and that he put the bottle in my locker. I don't like the sound of it someway and hustle the bottle down to the hobby shop, check, and beneath the yellow paint is about a lid of grass in a plastic bag.

I stash it in the garbage for temporary but on the way back to the barracks run into the dude who copped it for me. He wants a couple joints for his trouble. I still don't like the sound of it but fair is fair so we go back to the garbage can in the hobby shop and the paint bottle is <u>gone</u>! Hmmm. All very weird. An all-round day for getting ripped: good old Gordon comes up, his already stuck-out neck stuck out for his goodbuddy me and I get burned for my goods. Who was the alleycat snatched my cream?

Some **WISHES** do come true. Though I get burned on the dope I get to see family and they bring all kinds of **SOUND** equipment and **COLOR** which I take to the tailor shop. It's a little slow at the shop. Especially with all the action up at the barracks. So I close up and head for my bunk area.

A man don't hang around the office on Sundays; he goes home. Or to facsimile thereof.

I'm bunked in what is called the "high side" of the barracks. The staff says it's called high side because the numbers on the other sides are lower (I'm bunk #98; there are only 99 beds in camp so I'm next to last). The Bloods say it's called the high side of the barracks because it <u>is</u> the high side.

Breems' people have brought up his stereo and sides—Temptations, Miracles, Ray Charles, Lou Rawls . . . and there's music playing and dope circulating after a beautiful visiting day even tho some asshole has ripped off my lid of grass so all I got is the sack full of lollipops Jenny and Paula, my "cousins," brought up. And Chandler, Our Flower Child, has loaned me his genuine brass Russian Orthodox incense burner to set on my locker seeing as they confiscated all his incense . . . So I stick the lollipops in the holes. (**By the <u>also</u> way** . . . did you know that genuine imported expensive authentic Frankincense smells exactly like <u>hashish</u>?)

One of the Bloods drops by to check my lollipop display. Guy named Golden, called Goldie, small banty build and with a quiet shy look that lets you know better. He and his brother are doing a year "for 'molestin' the po-lees ya know?"

He studies my arrangement a moment over my shoulder, then asks, "You got a color there for me?"

"Don't know, let me check." I consider the selection and choose a deep purple to slip into his dark hand. He looks at it seriously. I wait for him to speak. We've never had much to do with each other before and I wonder why the interest; probably my helping Breems with a broken speaker on his phonograph. I remember Goldie was watching me silently as I worked. Finally I ask, "Purple do?"

He grins and says "That'll be fine, Home." **You got <u>any</u> idea what** <u>it's like</u> to be <u>new</u> in a prison barracks and have a young bad colored dude call you "**HOME**?" It's very close to being called "Brother."

Goldie takes the purple and also a green and leaves. And when he leaves there's two reds (psst: a red is dope jargon for a Seconal) lying on my lockertop beside the brass chain, and a tight white joint sticking from the incense hole where the purple lollipop had been. As he passes Breems' bunk he tosses the green lollipop to Breems, who's changing the record.

"Have a sucker, motherfucker."

Dear Babbs:

What's it like? Is it like this kind of Pen? or another? Who knows? (Well of course everybody does but etc.)

Anyway there's me and West and Porter working over the yesterday green sheet. "Who ran in that race?" "Oh, let me see. Damascus."

So they bet packs on a race already run and they don't find out the race results (fair's fair) until next day's paper. Learn a lot about the Big Game in slam like how to hold your mud over a bad call. The good players are the ones can turn out top performance even under a barrage of unjust shit. Some of the deputies are damned good at these shit barrages.

I'm bunked on what is called the "High side of the Barracks." The staff says it's called High side because the numbers on the other side are lower (I'm bunk #94; there are only #96 beds in camp so I'm next to last) The Bloods say it's cause this side of the Barracks is the High Side. Because Morton's people bring up his stereo and sides, Temptations, Miracles, Ray Charles, Lou Rawls and there's dope circulating after a beautiful visiting day and music playing and motherfuckers rapping at each other and some asshole has ripped me for the lid of grass Gordon smuggled in to me and all I got is the sack full of lollypops Jenny and Paula, my "cousins", brought up.

And Whitfield, Our Flower Child, has loaned me his genuine brass Russian Orthodox Incense burner to sit on my locker seeing as they confiscated his incense ...So I stick the lollypops in the holes.

By the Way...ALSO did you know that genuine imported expensive authentic Frankincense + Myrre smells exactly like HASH?

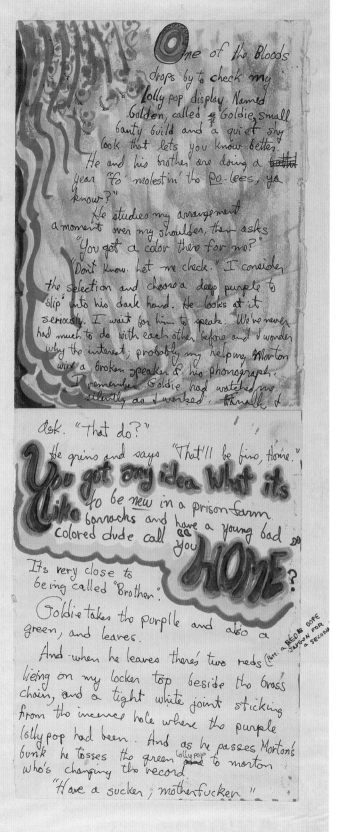

One of the Bloods drops by to check my lollypop display. Named Golden, called Goldie, small banty build and a quiet shy look that lets you know better.

He and his brother are doing a year "fo' molestin' the Po-lees, ya know?"

He studies my arrangement a moment over my shoulder, then asks "You got a color there for me?"

"Don't know. Let me check." I consider the selection and choose a deep purple to slip into his dark hand. He looks at it seriously. I wait for him to speak. We've never had much to do with each other before and I wonder why the interest; probably my helping Morton wire a broken speaker to his phonograph. I remember Goldie had watched me silently as I worked, finally, &

ask. "That do?"

He grins and says "That'll be fine, Home."

You got any idea what its like to be new in a prison farm barracks and have a young bad colored dude call you HOME?

It's very close to being called "Brother".

Goldie takes the purple and also a green, and leaves.

And when he leaves there's two reds (Att. a RED IS DOPE JARGON FOR A SECOND) lieing on my locker top beside the brass chain, and a tight white joint sticking from the incense hole where the purple lollypop had been. And as he passes Morton's bunk he tosses the green lollypop to Morton who's changing the record

"Have a sucker, motherfucker."

There's this Wayne, old USMC sergeant that never lightens up an ounce on me, yet some way conveys that it is for my betterment and not just grinding his ax (as is the case with most of the deputies) so he spooks me continually but, well, you know.

They had all the men who had visitors take an alky breather today. All neg. And one deputy dropped by yesterday asked me completely straight, "Are you loaded on something?" I told him no but that I've had this, well, this dizziness that is somewhat like being loaded . . . and so forth. So they can feel something happening and all they can figure is booze or dope. Even the inmates, all whispering, nudging each other, "Hey man, you got any stuff?" Only nobody does. At least any stuff you can put your finger on.

But there's some that know. You can tell by the twinkle of mischief in the eye. For example there's Sylvester, this absolutely formidable Blood with a knife scar gashed from his hairline to his collarbone right across his right eye. He knows. And this brain injury intellectual 17-year-old, he knows but can't believe it beyond J.R.R. Tolkien. And of course Page. And the big dumb 8-years-of-service-as-a-marine-DI deputy who reminds me of my wrestling coach and has an ulcer to boot, he knows real good—like a man been whomped between the eyes with a 40-lb Bible and hasn't cleared out the daze. He's the facility's main sergeant and the camp heavy, and is gonna have the toughest struggle of all reconciling what he knows in his heart with what he's had hammered into him in the corps. He's a gorilla, but he's a gorilla with a nightingale's heart.

And if I'm reading the handwriting on the wall correctly I think this gorilla is soon going to terminate my time in the tailor shop. The writing was on the wall when the wall turned orange. So my easy time days may be numbered. It seems I once more have pushed it until it popped. When will I learn?

Love, Keez

Dear Faye:

Page finally made it up, after seven weeks in the tank. Much glad to see him; say what you will about Page you got to admit he's noisy, and that's what's needed up here, a little beat. Also Zorro, remember? Just beginning to serve time on that assault charge—remember, a year or so ago when they were avenging Lovely Larry? Always glad to see an Angel; if only for the rubber ants they afford me. Also Paul Robertson was up, tired and looking a little stupid; not much hope for modification yet, he figures. But he's still working on a mistrial against Judge Di Mateus. He totes a fierce load of rationalization. I want him to get his group up here to play.

Also two reporters in two days; Mrs. Paine from *Old Oregon* yesterday (Local Boy Makes Good) and Burton Wolfe today doing research on the Hippies for the *Chronicle*. All very diplomatic and weighty and fucking exhausting. All sorts of people have now got me to hold still so they can ask me a few questions. Like "What's it feel like to swim?" "Well, first you get wet." "Wet? What's wet?" "Wet? Oh, you know; it's sorta, well, uh, er . . ." But you don't dare toss a bucket of water in their face, because you can never tell when one's got an itchy trigger finger. So it's go slow, so slow.

(The brothers Blood cease their dominoes a moment to toast a spider with a lighter. The brothers White's noses all wrinkle at the barbarism—"Not a spider with a lighter!")

Lights out in the dorm; the graveyard shift moves into the dayroom. Dominoes give way to moody letter writers and *Reader's Digest* readers . . .

Visiting day is a frustration. (The sewage disposal tone is off tonight for some unknown reason; our E-sharp is missing. The natives are restless.) One sometimes forgets that it's happening likewise on both ends. And in that faithless forgetting, allows Old Dog Doubt (—and it's just at this moment, synchronisitacklety, Speedy Lopez, our UFO from over the border, zooms through the dayroom, clacking mexurmericanese) a chance to creep slowly in.

Well there's one character we don't have to worry about creeping slowly in— Speedy Lopez. Speedy don' do nothin slow. He's a tough little Mexican mongrel the sort that drives Ol' Doubt crazy . . . about 35, looks 45, lean as a twist of jerky. They busted him just as he was banging up in a East Palo motel, took him to jail but he was jabbering so unbridled non-stop that the nightpatrol at the jail refused to take him in. "Haul this noisy asshole up to camp—serve 'em both right."

They released him into C Barracks just before lights out. "We've got a little UFO for you lucky sonsaguns," Rhack informs us.

They open the rear of the paddy wagon and this rawhide cyclone hits the ground spinning, eyes red-rimmed with devilment and grin bleeding at the corners. "Heyee, muchachos! Mi yamma Speedy LOPEZ SPEEDY Lopez! All dey got on me is I like to shoot crank and eat POOZEE shoot crank and eat POOZEE can you DEEG IT?!"

Listen. I hear Con, our German shepherd, barking at the gimpy coon off in the woods. Con wandered into camp half dead from a week-long deer chase with no food and the men pulled him back to health. Nice dog for a German shepherd. Coon doesn't have a tail, lost it under a garbage can lid. We also got a cat named Fruit and he don't like Con or Coon. One big snappy family.

luv, ken

AS YOU FILE THROUGH THE DOOR, TAKE ONE OF THE FOLDING CHAIRS ARRANGED IN TWO LARGE CIRCLES, ONE INSIDE THE OTHER.

NOBODY NONE TO HAPPY AT THE PROSPECT. THE CLOCK CLICKS TO TWO O'CLOCK. A DEPUTY LOOKS AT ONE OF THE PRISONERS. "OKAY, THIS MEETING IS NOW CALLED TO ORDER," THE PRISONER SAYS.

SILENCE. ONE MINUTE. TWO MINUTES.

"LETS HAVE THE NEW MEN STAND UP AND INTRODUCE THEM-SELVES."

WE DO.

"THIS IS ONE OF OUR BI-WEEKLY GROUP MEETINGS. YOU MEN HAVE THE OPPORTUNITY TO CONFRONT EACH OTHER OR MEMBERS OF THE STAFF IN THESE MEETINGS, AIR SOME GRIEVANCES, GET SOME THINGS OFF YOUR CHEST. WHAT IS SAID IN THESE MEETINGS IS TO STAY IN THESE MEETINGS. WE TRY TO BE HONEST WITH EACH OTER, SHOOT FROM THE SHOULDER, TELL THE STAFF HOW YOU REALLY FEEL... WITHOUT FEAR OF CONSEQUENCE."

A CYNICAL LAUGH DRAWS ATTENTION. BUT SINCE THE LAUGH COMES FROM A SECTION WHERE THE BLOODS SIT TOGETHER GHETTO-LIKE, ITS IMPOSSIBLE TO PINPOINT THE LAUGHER. THE DEPUTY GOES ON:

"I KNOW SOME OF YOU DON'T BELIEVE THIS YET, BUT THEN SOME OF US DON'T BELIEVE IT EITHER. THIS CAMP IS AN EXPERIMENT, YOU SEE, AND WE THINK, A PRETTY SUCCESSFUL ONE. WITH A LITTLE WORK ON EVERYBODY'S PART, A LITTLE CO-OPERATION AND HONESTY, I--WE-- THINK IT CAN BE DAMNED SUCCESSFUL AND THIS DREAM OF REHABILITATION CAN WORK!"

AGAIN THAT LAUGH, FOLLOWED THIS TIME BY THE SARGEANT'S HIGH IRRITATED VOICE: "WE CAN ALSO MAKE THINGS A LOT TOUGHER!"

At exactly 2:30 Mr. Buckner opened the meeting by introducing the new men in camp. Mr. Campbell woke up, by explaining one of the rules, that the men on the bus should obey, but is usual

BiGroup

GROUP SNIVEL

"ALL RIGHT THE MEETING IS NOW OPEN EVERYBODY SHUT UP!"

Deputy Brazil stands at the door of the mess hall with a roster on a clipboard, checking off your bunk number as you file through the door, take one of the folding chairs arranged in two large circles, one inside the other. Nobody none too happy at the prospect. The clock clicks to two o'clock. The Deputy looks at one of the prisoners. "Okay, this meeting is now called to order. Start talking."

The prisoner blinks and yawns. Silence. One minute. Two minutes.

"Okay then, let's have the new men stand up and introduce themselves."

We do.

"Okay, this is one of our bi-weekly group meetings. You men have the opportunity to confront each other or members of the staff in these meetings, air some grievances, get some things off your chest. What is said in these meetings is to stay in these meetings. We try to be honest with each other, shoot from the hip, straight from the shoulder, tell the staff how you <u>really</u> feel . . . without fear of consequence."

A cynical laugh draws attention. But since the laugh comes from the section where the Bloods sit together ghetto-like, it's impossible to pinpoint the source. The deputy goes on:

"I know some of you don't believe this yet, but then some of us don't believe it either. This camp is an experiment, you see, and we think a pretty successful one. With a little work on everybody's part, a little cooperation and honesty, I—we—think it can be damn successful and this dream of rehabilitation can <u>work</u>!"

Again the laugh. Followed this time by the deputy's high irritated voice: "We can also make things a lot tougher!"

> Group minutes:
> At exactly 2:00 Dpt. Brazil opens the meeting by introducing the new men in camp. Then Mr. Fassenaux wakes up by explaining one of the rules that the men must obey but is usually—
>
> "—concerning the hobby shop," Srgt. Crosssfield says, "and a couple other things in the camp. I feel there is a slight tension between the deputies and inmates." Some people don't like the way the hobby shop is painted at present and he suggests that the hobby shop should be repainted more conventional.

Suddenly my beautiful hobby-and-tailor shop is in jeopardy. "Conventional how?" I ask.

"Conventional gray."

"Gray?" the group gasps, stunned. Me too.

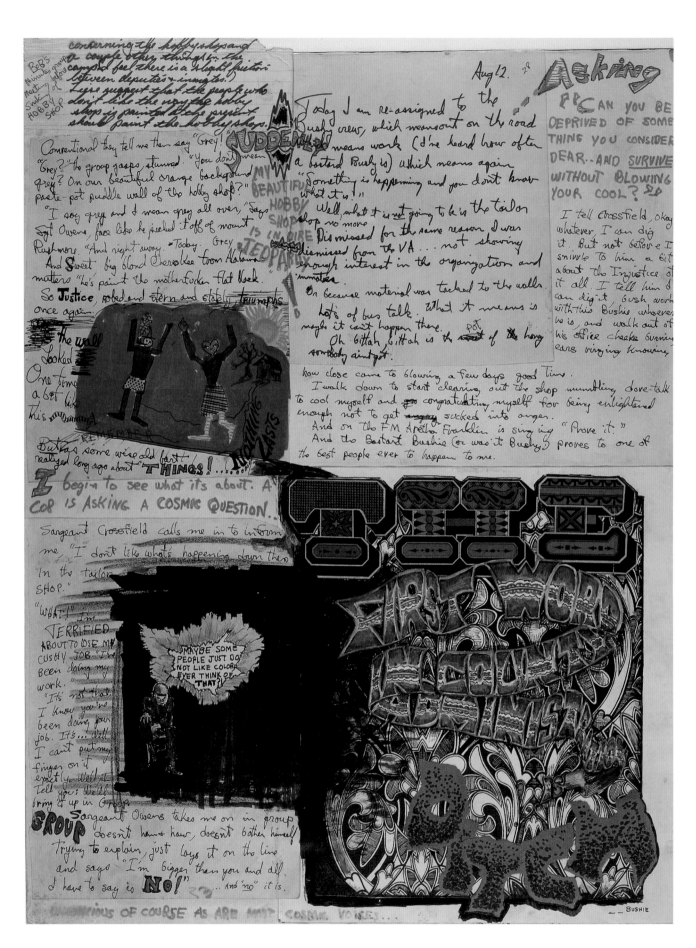

(Bob's Minute group before Sunkey HOBBY SHOP)

concerning the hobby-shops and of course other things in the camp... I feel there is a slight friction between deputies + inmates.)

Lige suggest that the people who don't like the way the hobby shop is painted the present should paint the hobby-shops.

Conventional they tell me then say "Grey!" "Grey?" the group gasps, stunned. "You don't mean grey? On our beautiful orange background paste-pot puddle wall of the hobby shop?"

"I say grey and I mean grey all over," says Sgt Owens, face like he picked it off of mount Rushmore. "And right away. Today. Grey."

And Sweet, big blond Cherokee toon Alabama matters "he's paint the motherfucker flat black."

So Justice, robed and stern and stately triumphs once again.

SUDDENLY MY BEAUTIFUL HOBBY SHOP IS IN DIRE JEOPARDY!

The wall looked

One time a bit like this

REMEMBER NOTHING LASTS

But as some wise old fart realized long ago about "THINGS!... NOTHING LASTS"

I begin to see what its about. A COP IS ASKING A COSMIC QUESTION..

Sergeant Crossfield calls me in to inform me, "I don't like what's happening down there in the tailor SHOP."

"WHAT!" I'm TERRIFIED ABOUT TO LOSE MY CUSHY JOB. "I've been doing my work."

"It's not that. I know you've been doing your job. It's... Well I can't put my finger on it exactly. Well I Tell you: Will bring it up in Group.

GROUP Sargeant Owens takes me on in group doesn't hem haw, doesn't bother himself trying to explain, just lays it on the line and says "I'm bigger than you and all I have to say is **NO!**"... And "no" it is.

VICTORIOUS OF COURSE AS ARE ALL COSMIC VOICES...

Aug 12.

ASKING

Today I am re-assigned to the Bushy crew, which means out on the road which means work (I've heard how often a bastard Bushy is) which means again "Something is happening and you don't know what it is."

Well, what it is not going to be is the tailor shop no more.

Dismissed for the same reason I was dismissed from the VA... not showing enough interest in the organization and inmates.

Or because material was tacked to the walls.

Lots of bus talk. What it means is maybe it can't happen there. pot

Oh bittah, bittah is the root of the long somebody aint got.

how close came to blowing a few days good Time.

I walk down to start clearing out the shop mumbling dove-talk to cool myself and congratulating myself for being enlightened enough not to get sucked into anger.

And on the FM Aretha Franklin is singing "Prove it."

And the Bastard Bushie (or was it Bushy) proves to one of the best people ever to happen to me.

CAN YOU BE DEPRIVED OF SOMETHING YOU CONSIDER DEAR.. AND SURVIVE WITHOUT BLOWING YOUR COOL?

I tell Crossfield, okay whatever I can dig it. But not before I snivvle to him a bit about the Injustice of it all. I tell him I can dig it, Gush work with this Bushie whoever he is, and walk out of his office cheeks burning ears ringing knowing

MAYBE SOME PEOPLE JUST DO NOT LIKE COLOR EVER THINK OF THAT?!

FIRST WORD

BUSHIE

"You don't mean gray?" Fassenaux asks. "I for one just can't see gray over our beautiful orange background pastepot puddle wall of a hobby shop."

"I see gray and I mean gray all over," says Sergeant Wayne, face like he picked it up off Mount Rushmore. "And right away. Today. Gray."

And Sweet, the big blond half Cherokee half racist from Alabama mutters, "Le's paint the motherfucker flat black."

So justice, robed and stern and stately, triumphs once again.

But remember, as some wise old fart realized long ago about things . . . nothing lasts.

I begin to see what it's all about. A cop is asking a cosmic question. When Sergeant Crossfield called me in yesterday to inform me, "I don't like what's happening down there in the tailor shop—" it was actually a cosmic question: "What are you made of, Kesey?"

Of jello, apparently, by the way I start shaking—scared I'm about to lose my cushy position. "How come? I've been doing my job—"

"It's not that. I know you've been doing your job. It's that . . . well it's that I can't put my finger on it exactly. Well I tell you; we'll bring it up in group." In group Sergeant Wayne takes me on—doesn't hem and haw, doesn't bother himself trying to explain, just lays it on the line between the lines, saying in effect I'm bigger than you and all I have to say is no . . . so no it is.

"Maybe some people just do not like color, Mr. Kesey. Ever think of that?"

Today I'm assigned to the Bushie crew, which means out on the road which means work (I'd heard often how bad a slave driver Bushie is) which means again "something is happening and you don't know what it is."

Well, I know one thing it is. I'm not going to be in the tailor shop no more. Dismissed for the same reason I was dismissed from my nurse's aide job at the Palo Alto VA hospital: "not showing enough interest in the inmates or respect for the institution." Or because colorful materials was tacked to the walls. Lots of bus talk. Lots of it can't happen here not in this institution whatever the hell it is.

Oh bittah, bittah is the pot of honey, sonny, you ain't got.

—The cosmic question un-asked but asking "Can you be deprived of something you consider dear—and survive without blowing your cool?"

I go to Wayne's office after group and turn in my hobby shop key and tell him hey, whatever, I can dig it—(but not before I snivel to him a bit about the injustice of it all, snif snif)—I can dig it, doing bush work with this bastard Bushie whoever he is!—and walk out of his office, cheeks burning ears ringing knowing how close I came to blowing up at him and blowing a few days good time.

I walk down to start cleaning the shop mumbling dove-talk to cool off and congratulating myself on being enlightened enough not to get sucked into anger. And on FM Aretha Franklin is singing "Prove it." And the bastard Bushie (or is it Bushy) proves to be one of the best people ever to happen to me.

IN THE BUSH WITH BUSHIE

SWEET sunset sunset sunset sunset
dogs barking around the bush after birds

Dear Faye: Hi. How's life on the streets? I lost my fine tailor shop job. Why? Same old reason. Making waves. Using too

much

COLOR

Just when I was getting good at it, too.

However, I have been promoted. To a digger of ditches dig dig dig dig dig.

It's a healthy change of business. Building roads and culverts for a small county park. Trail is on our crew. Also Goldie, the lead Blood from our barracks.

Our boss is an old white-haired fart known as Bushie. A retired county works supervisor come outta retirement to offer his expertise to young hellbents don't know one end of the shovel from t'other. Pretty good at it, too. He showed me how I was supposed to hold a handsaw: "Hold it like it was a gun butt, keeping that pointing finger pointed straight down the saw like it was a gun barrel. And don't cut on the push cut on the <u>pull</u>!"

Made sawing about ten times easier.

Trail asks "Mr. Bushie?"—in that sweet snow-the-boss voice—"How does a man rise in county work? Say for example into administration?"

"Well Mr. Trail," Bushie answers, just as sweet—"The first word in county administration is 'ditch.'"

Now I'm at the work furlough facility. Jerk furlough, as Rhack calls it. They don't know if they want me or not. Leastways not in striped shoes. So I'm gonna try to get hold of my suit and shoes and stuff. I think they may be at Rohan's.

Sitting here in the library with Trail (whose son's name is Mark and comes from up above Tillamook).

Across the road the buzz of model planes goes on past lights-out. Cars hiss up Bayshore. Lights hum. Toilets flush. Men whisper. Bloods laugh under their lips, dark secret syrup-sound that has been the battle-cry of the Psychedelic Fascist long before the word Fascist was heard of, let alone psychedelic . . . the cry of "I can dig it, massa, but can <u>you</u> dig it?"

I seem to have a pretty good counselor here, a lot like Givens at camp . . . healthy, tolerant and realistic, rare qualities in a cop.

The pace is faster here. The beat far heavier. Trail comes in, gives me half his 7-Up. I still don't know if I'll get out on the *Chronicle* gig or not, so I'm not counting on it. But the staff has indicated that my chances are far better if I don't wear striped shoes. I think the real

IN THE BUSH WITH BUSHIE

TRAIL ASKS BUSHIE, "MR. BUSHIE?" — IN THAT SWEET SHOW VOICE FOR THE BOSS — "HOW DOES A MAN RISE IN COUNTY WORK? SAY FOR EXAMPLE INTO ADMINISTRATION?"

"WELL, MR. TRAIL," BUSHIE ANSWERS JUST AS SWEET — "THE FIRST WORD IN COUNTY ADMINISTRATION IS DITCH."

SWEET

:HI.
I LOST MY FINE
TAILOR SHOP
Just when I was getting good at it, too
HOWEVER I HAVE BEEN

USING TOO MUCH

DIG DIG DIG DIG DIG TO A DIGGER OF DITCHES.

KESEY SMCO #2 REDWOOD CITY, CALIF.

How's life on the street? JOB. WHY? SAME OLD REASON. MAKING MONEY AND

HEALTHY BUSINESS. BUILDING ROADS AND CULVERTS FOR A SMALL COUNTY PARK. TRAIL ON OUR CREW. ALSO GOLDIE, THE LITTLE SPADE FROM OUR BARRACKS. OUR BOSS IS AN OLD WHITE-HAIRED FART KNOWN

41

hang-up however is Judge Di Mateus. He told Paul, "I want Kesey to do six months. If I'd wanted him on the street I wouldn't have sentenced him to jail." So . . . we'll wait and not plan on it.

After talking to you today I'd give five (days, that is) to see you. "Ain't that phone a motherfucker!" says Trail after talking with his wife (another Oregon girl) and having the same reaction. A telephone and a lot of Coke and candy machines out in the breezeway and he goes through four bucks a day. "Ain't this a drag; you got to go to work to support these lousy machines."

Don't try to make it down until the doctor thinks you're up to it.

Love, Ken

The Kesey Style

My parole officer Duggs arrives at about 10. Looking mighty grim and longfaced. "The Powers That Be say 'no' to work furlough."

He hasn't even seen the "Kesey Style" article in the *Chronicle* with the picture of me and the tailor shop wall. Gives no reason why I was shot down from work furlough. Doesn't need to. We talk. His face is heavy under its thin look. Dirt too deep down for any detergent to touch. Any ordinary detergent, that is.

"It's a dirty deal," he consoles.

"Yeah," I agree.

But can you dig it, Duggs; will you ever be able to dig it? Or are you buried so deep so long in it that it'll take another's shovel to save you.

And does anybody dig you enough to dig you out?

"Well . . . I tried."

"Thanks, Duggs."

So now it's do time and wait to be moved.

Be strong and hold your mud a month and ruefully-gleefully watch the shit boil and bubble. Stirring secretly on occasion, just to keep it interesting.

All right! Enough civil-farting around. Look up yonder. That's Charles Trail coming bare-chested, bronze and beautiful out of the trees. As choice a specimen of young American manhood as ever hefted an ax. Polite, hard-working, handsome. Doing a year for rape.

Brrszzwang**gggg**! Khzzzzw**anG**! We're in the bush with Bushie clearing bush for a proposed park, tossing the chopped brush through the chipper. **Zhr**wan**gggG**! The chipper is an angry deathdrive monster with an insatiable appetite **grrRRINGGgg**!

When feeding the chipper you have to wear <u>gloves</u> because of the thorns and <u>poison oak</u> and <u>goggles</u> and a <u>mask</u> because of the dust. And if you don't feed it fast enough it winds up till it sounds like it's gonna eat itself. We've already lost a couple of gloves through it, be just as easy to lose an arm. There's things I'd rather do than feed the chipper.

"Those on medication or gets poison oak best do the falling and chopping and stay off the chipper," Bushie says. I'm taking Librium and Trail is notorious for poison oak.

"Sir, you won't believe this, but when I worked on that chipper during your vacation I was in bed <u>three days.</u>" Trail fingers his ax handle like Honest Abe Lincoln.

But <u>Bushie</u> doesn't believe it, matter of fact—you can tell by his slow study of Trail's innocent face—but he gives us axes and sends us both uphill to chop and drag brush. Goldie and Rivera get blessed with the job of feeding the monster. They give us hard looks as we leave.

Trail works like a bastard for a few minutes, then, when we both get a respectable sweat up, we ease off and rap about hunting. His wife's from Oregon, the coast country. We've both hunted duck and elk in the same area. Played football and wrestled against the same high schools. We finally get around to running our beefs down to each other.

" . . . You won't believe this, but she blew the whistle on us for <u>no other reason</u> than I wouldn't <u>scarf the box</u>! On a <u>bunch</u> of us! But Joe and me copped to it so they'd let our other cousins go."

Joe is Trail's cousin, another bright good-looking all-American boy with a bummed leg. Quiet. He bunks in A Barracks he's so quiet.

"Our lawyer told us we'd get a deal—probation—seeing as she wasn't hurt. When that judge said a year I swear to God, Ken, I thought I was having some kind of nightmare."

As he talks I begin to get the feeling I'm being <u>hustled</u> and I don't know for what.

"But I <u>wasn't</u> gonna eat that bitch—not after half a dozen other guys had screwed her!"

I sympathize, telling him about various Hell's Angels sex raps that are like his—"Some chick thinks she can do the <u>whole Angel</u> thing and about half-way through a chapter she gets scared or sore and freaks and hollers rape . . ."

"This wasn't like that though, Ken. To be perfectly honest, I'd already screwed her once and was ready to leave. But <u>Joe</u> hadn't screwed her. She said she'd let Joe screw her if <u>I'd</u> eat her and, well, we argued, and I kind of had to <u>hold</u> her for Joe. That's what the DA made such a big deal about; me sitting on her <u>head</u>! Like I was on a <u>sadist</u> trip. And all the papers played it all big: sex fiend. Because I wouldn't eat her."

It was the old I-got-a-raw-deal snivel that we all sing one time or another. I believed the story, pretty much—with the same hesitation Bushie had.

Trail and I worked together all that week telling street stories. Under his cover he's smart and sensitive, and basically as honest as his front advertises (not that he believed the ad; few of us do). And I liked working with him. We talked about our strengths (how many matches won, women laid) and our weaknesses. "All dope," I expanded my current theory, "is relative. I like to get loaded! When I let it come my way that's one thing, but when I get strung up with <u>desire</u> for it, that's another. <u>That's</u> dope."

"Ken . . ." He glanced back and forth, eased up close and confidential. "You notice how many shits I've taken today? Well, every Thursday I start getting a case of the runs. Now I'm going to tell you something nobody but Joe knows. At noon, this Friday, <u>tomorrow</u> . . . my wife parks down the road about two miles. I run down and meet her and run back."

"That's what you mean by runs?"

"No! No!" He was completely serious. "That's so the work supervisor doesn't get suspicious when I'm gone all lunch break; he thinks I'm shitting."

"But <u>two miles</u>?"

"I don't want her getting caught. I've got it down perfect." He shook his head. "We've been doing it every Friday since I came out on this crew," he said, helplessly.

"Dope's dope," I said, philosophically.

"There's nothing I can do about it."

Then later that afternoon he felled a tree on my head.

Which shakes a lot of stuff loose. Like the big group snivel that night. New Blood asks "What's these meetin' s'posed to be about?" And Deputy Rhack shoots it right to me: "Tell him would you, Mr. Kesey? What it's all about?"

I knew better. I'd managed to keep my mouth shut pretty much in previous meetings, as all the old-timer cons had advised. But that tree had shook loose my con armor and TRUTH was clambering for some fresh air. And up it came. For 45 minutes I held the room spellbound with thought-stream pyrotechnics, word salad, parables, esoteria, and even some cosmic bullshit. And Trail sitting beside me nudging, prodding and doing everything but clap his hand over my mouth. I finally got the hint and wound it up.

"—and that, Mr. Rhack, is what it's all about!"

I heard Trail groan and I realized I'd made a mistake.

That tree had set off a whole chain of events to rattle my head. The next day, Trail had his morning's bowel problem as predicted and was gone so long at lunch break that I was sent into the woods to find him. He was just coming up the trail, glistening with sweat and glowing like a Greek god.

"You look like you really got smoothed out."

For an answer he broke into "<u>Some Enchanted Eveningggg</u>!" in a lovely tenor. I went green with envy: Jesus would I like a joint!

Trail continued to sing as the afternoon passed, and about three o'clock Bushie gave me my chance. "Who wants to take a ride?" He was going to take the 10-wheeler up to the watertank to cut some overhang. Easy work compared to the chipper and of course everyone wanted to take a ride. Someone has to stay to keep at this brush pile. He starts naming off guys he wants for a crew—Goldie, Jones, Kirby—and I get an idea.

"Mr. Bushie, I'd as leave stay. I got a little headache and I don't think that 10-wheeler'd help it. Let Golden go."

"Fine plan," Goldie agreed. Zoom, they're gone. Us left-behinds shut down the chipper and settle back to loaf. It's sunny and there's a nice breeze.

Now, across the highway are some houses I've had my eyes on for some time. When I lived in La Honda all those houses used to be infested with heads. So after a couple complaints about my aching skull I announce I'm going across the street after aspirin. I troop up to the first likely looking cottage (Wasn't I at a party here a couple years back? With smokin dope ankle-deep?) and knock on the door. Wait. I hear somebody. Knock again. They're taking so long it's bound to be a bunch of stoned hippies honored to lay a lid on me. Then . . . blah. A little old rosy-cheeked lady about 65. I give her the bit about the tree and the headache, tell her I'm from the sheriff's honor camp and could I have a few aspirin?

"Goodness me, you're not from the place where they got that dope fiend Kesey, are you?" Her words, s'help me God. And since I'm always courteous to a fan and a little addled anyway I answer, "As a matter of fact, I <u>am</u> that dope fiend Kesey."

Not the wisest thing I've ever done, but the little old lady is delighted. Invites me in to talk with the old man while she hunts me up some special painkillers. Her husband is a paraplegic with the same rosy-cheeked good humor, propped up in bed with his old gnarled root hanging into an aluminum bedpan.

"Put that thing away," she scolds, pulling the sheets up over his groin.

"Nothin' the boy hasn't seen before," pulling the sheet back with a fly swatter. He gives me a big wink: "Man gotta see everything comin' out all right, don't he?"

We rap awhile. The old couple is delighted to have company. I get more and more antsy. She offers me some homemade berry wine, I refuse: "Against the rules."

"Oh. Of course."

Finally say I'd better head back (hoping to still try one of the other cottages) but she got to rummage after the aspirin again. And the old man wants to know all about "this here LSD stuff."

I finally leave with a handful of Emprin and a promise to bring them some of our brush for kindling wood when I return, and sprint back just in time to see the 10-wheeler returning. Kirby, a hype with a lot of joint time, is no more fooled by my headache than he was by Trail's shits: "Get anything?"

"Just some pain pills. The hippies who used to live there have split." He examines one of the pills, bites it, gives it back with a grin. "Don't look like you did as good as old Trail."

AND HERE COMES TRAIL bronze arms spread to the afternoon sun, chest thrust into the breeze, legs spread to absorb the bounce of the 10-wheeler, his all-American voice lifting above the spired redwoods: "—and when you see . . . those Golden Ear-rings . . ."

Then snap all his talk about cousins, and roofing jobs, and barn painting, plus his built-in hustling innocence . . . all of it clicks together. But it's not quite snapshot sharp: he doesn't know I know. The picture doesn't finish developing until Sunday.

Back in camp and glory, glory, there's a tape recorder and flute. "Your wife's two cousins brought them up this afternoon," Sergeant Wayne tells me. "They said they'd be up for a picnic this coming Sunday with your brother."

Hot damn! A tape recorder! And my flute! And Chuck and who know's who else coming up! And the work week over! And a movie tonight! Glory and yes!

I flute a little celebration, with Page on the guitar. I notice the flute doesn't quite fit back into its case like it ought to. Page and I take it into his little shack at the pool and rip out the blue velvet lining and Hot Double Damn! There's four STP tabs, couple of psilocybin pills and five good old Owsley purples!—my favorite of all the Owsley vintages. Perfect for this pastoral setting. Purples I always associate with Mexico and the lush, jungle highs spent there; other higher frequency batches like white lightnings or flying saucers would have been too heavy for me during incarceration. Even more so would have been a full STP trip—eek! (Page and I just nibbled those during our stay. STP in jail would be like STP on Haight Street: a hard work trip and no work to trip into. The reason, I think, for so many bummers on this drug, is when you swallow 30 hours of pure energy you better have more on hand to do than to sniff incense and read the *Oracle*.)

FRIDAY NIGHT and SOME DUDE

out of THE BLUE HAS RIPPED Breems for the needle out of his stereo . . . rendering C Barracks silent and putting the Bloods up pretty tight. So Page and I take the recorder down to Page's pool-maintenance shack and tape his James Brown album. Page wants to turn on right now. But I want to wait for Trail, see if he'd like a crack at some new dope.

Page don't like the idea. "I don't think he can hold his mud behind acid."

"I think he can. About half a cap. There's more to him than he's got out front"—and we take the tape and player back up to the barracks.

would have taken a week or better. A little piece of information on behalf of a useful but much-maligned (dope.)

low and very slow and watches Liso and Grooms with the super-cool benevolence of the older Negro patiently waiting for the young bucks to wise up. Finally says "Liso..." ..like a note blown across a big black jug.. "What *is it ex-act-ly..you are in here for?"

Liso says "I in the county jail, sir, for goin' too fast... for steppin' too quick... and for not bein' too cool." Then goes at Grooms

with a karate stance "Haw!" Grooms returns gesture "Haw!" Liso makes a swipe "Eee YAW!"

"Bitch! You kicked me with those big brogans! Almost break my blue glasses..."

Bland sniffs at the whole performance: "Buncha wet-nosed cock lickers." obviously pleased with the way the younger generation is shaping up.

Chandler bouncing a tennis ball, flat-palmed like a kid in a comic strip, face as round as the ball he's bouncing.

Speedy Lopez swaggers through stirring instant coffee in a cup. Hits on his heels thump so loud reminds me how a chicken jumping from roost to floor hits with a thump ten times his size. And Speedy's hips and backbone working from a bad wreck in his youth. And his arms terrifically gnarled and knotted with muscles. A two-hundred pound Puerto Rican boiled down to his hundred pound peppery essence. "Speedy," Chandler calls, "how about a cup of coffee for me?"

"You kees my bleenking light!"

"You can bouree my bleenking ball...?"

James Brown sings "Sweet --- sweet Loraine"

Grooms, always heedless of words being played, sings his own: "Ooo little girl..." head back

RIGHT NOW. But I want to wait for Trail, see if he'd like a crack at some new dope. Page don't like the idea. "I don't think he can hold his mud behind acid."

"I think he can. About a half a cap. There's more to him than he's got out front."

We sit around the day room listening to James Brown, watching Liso and Grooms pantomime the words, playing with the pens Ed brought me (very popular item; our day room table is filled with Bloods sketching and doodling--looks like a CORE art class) and waiting for the Friday night flick to be announced.

Bland is tipped back in a chair, stocking feet on the table watching Liso and Grooms bop around. Bland is a straight-haired Blood, tall, good looking and probably Louisiana in his background. Talks very

and his mouth pink and obscene "...ooo little girl... can you dig me... out here in this moonlight.."

voice lifted to all the insensitive lovelies on that far off street.

...voice somewhere

We sit around the dayroom listening to James Brown, watching Liso and Breems pantomime the words, playing with the pens Ed brought me (very popular item; our dayroom table's filled with Bloods sketching and doodling—looks like a CORE art class)—passing time and waiting for the Friday night flick to be announced.

Bland is tipped back in a chair, stocking feet on the table watching Liso and Breems bop around. Bland is a straight-haired Blood, tall, good looking and probably got some Louisiana in his background. Talks very low and very slow and watches Liso and Breems with the super-cool benevolence of the older Negro patiently waiting for the young bucks to wise up. Finally says "Breems—?" . . . like a note blown across a big black jug. "What is it ex-act-ly . . . you are in here for?"

Breems says "I'm in the county jail, sir, for goin' too fast, stepping too quick . . . and for not bein' too cool." Then goes at Liso with a karate stance "Haw!" Liso returns the gesture "Haw!" and makes a swipe "Eeeeyaw!"

"Bitch! You kicked me with those big brogans! Almost break my blue glasses . . . "

Bland sniffs at the whole performance: "Bunch of wet-nosed cock lickers," obviously pleased with the way this younger generation is shaping up.

Chandler is bouncing a tennis ball, flat-palmed like a kid in a comic strip, face as round as the ball he's bouncing.

Speedy Lopez swaggers through stirring instant coffee in a cup. Hits his heels thump so loud reminds me how a chicken jumping from roost to floor hits with a thump ten times his size. And Speedy's hips and backbone working odd from a bad wreck in his youth. And his arms terrifically gnarled and knotted with muscles. A two-hundred pound fighting cock boiled down to his hundred-pound peppery essence. "Speedy," Chandler calls, "how about a cup of coffee for me?"

"You kees my bleenkin' light."

"You can bounce my bleenkin' ball."

James Brown sings "Sweet . . . Sweet Lorraine."

Breems, always heedless of words being sung, sings his own: "Ooo little girl . . . ."—head back and his mouth pink and obscene, "Ooo ooo little girl . . . can you dig me . . . out here in this moonlight . . . " voice lifted to all the insensitive lovelies on that far off street:

. . . voice somewhere

between Belafonte and Billy Daniels: "can you dig me . . . so shy . . . so sweet . . . so, so . . ." The world always playing accompaniment for Breems.

In fact, it's all so mellow that Page has forgotten about our stash and has tripped into a sign he is making for his pool . . . everybody just grooving . . . just Goofing and Grooving.

then . . . the tape breaks!

Just as Trail walks in with Sweet and Snyder. Uh-oh . . .

They've come from the weightroom all pumped up and fierce and CLANG VERY HEAVY (so heavy, in fact, I run outta black ink, have to mix this wunnerful substitute) (which is worse than no ink). Shit! Which aggravate me terrible. Oh, the conditions a true artist got to be submitted to.

between Belafonte & Billy Daniels: "Can you dig me...

So shy... so sweet... so, so..." The world always playing accompaniment for Grooms

In fact, its all so mellow that Page has forgotten about our stash and is tripped into a sign he's making for his pool... everybody just grooving...

...just Goofing and Grooving

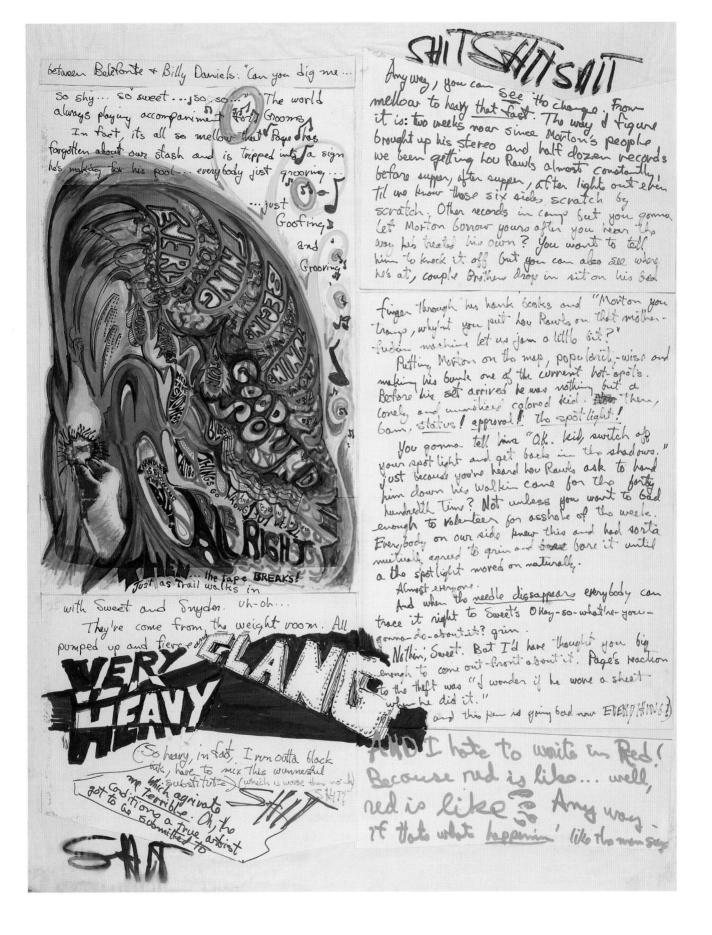

THEN... the tape BREAKS!
Just as Trail walks in

with Sweet and Snyder. uh-oh...

They've come from the weight room. All pumped up and fierce and CLANG

VERY HEAVY

(So heavy, in fact, I run outta black ink, have to mix this wunnerful substitute which agrivate me Terrible. Oh, the conditions a true artist got to be submitted to

SHIT SHIT SHIT

Any way, you can see the change. From mellow to heavy that fact. The way I figure it is: two weeks now since Morton's people brought up his stereo and half dozen records we been getting Lou Rawls almost constantly before supper, after supper, after lights out even til we know those six sides scratch by scratch. Other records in camp but you gonna let Morton borrow yours after you hear the way he's treated his own? You want to tell him to knock it off but you can also see where he's at, couple Brothers drop in sit on his bed

finger through his hank books and "Morton you trans, why'nt you put Lou Rawls on that mother-fuckin machine let us jam a little bit?"

Putting Morton on the map, popularity-wise and making his bunk one of the current hot-spots. Before his set arrives he was nothing but a lonely and unnoticed colored kid. Then, bam, status! approval! the spotlight!

You gonna tell him "OK. kid, switch off your spotlight and get back in the shadows." just because you've heard Lou Rawls ask to hand him down his walkin cane for the forty hundredth time? Not unless you want to God enough to volunteer for asshole of the week. Everybody on our side knew this and had sorta mutually agreed to grin and bare it until the spotlight moved on naturally.

Almost everyone.
And when the needle dissappears everybody can trace it right to Sweet's Okay-so-what're-you-gonna-do-about-it? grin.

Nothin, Sweet. But I'd have thought you big enough to come out-front about it. Page's reaction to the theft was "I wonder if he wore a sheet when he did it."

(and this pen is going bad now EVERYTHING)

AND I hate to write in Red! Because red is like... well, red is like? Any way - if that's what happenin' like the man say

SHIT SHIT SHIT

Anyway, you can <u>see</u> the change. From mellow to heavy <u>that fast</u>. The way I figure it is: two weeks now since Breems' people brought up his stereo and half a dozen records we been getting Lou Rawls almost constantly, before supper, after supper, after lights out even, til we know those six sides scratch by scratch. There are other records in camp, but you gonna let Breems borrow yours after you hear the way he's treated his own? You want to tell him to knock it off but you can also see where he's at: couple Brothers drop in sit on his bed finger through his hank books and say "Breems you tramp; why'nt you put Lou Rawls on that motherfuckin machine let us jam a little bit?"

Putting Breems on the camp map, popularity-wise, and making his bunk one of the current hot-spots. Before his stereo arrived he was nothing but a lonely and unnoticed kid. Then, bam, <u>status</u>! <u>approval</u>! <u>the spotlight</u>!

You gonna tell him "Okay kid, switch off your spotlight and get back in the shadows," just because you've heard Lou Rawls sing "Hand Me Down My Walking Cane" for the forty hundredth time? Not unless you want to bad enough to volunteer for asshole of the week. Everybody on our side of C Barracks knew this and had sorta mutually agreed to grin and bear it until the spotlight moves on naturally.

Almost everybody.

And when the <u>needle disappears</u> everybody can trace it back to Sweet's Okay-so-what're-you-gonna-do-about-it? musclebound grin.

(Nothin', Sweet, nothing—especially with you pumped-up big fresh from the iron pile. But one would've thought you woulda been big enough to come out front about it . . .)

(Page's reaction to the theft was "I wonder if he wore a sheet when he did it.")

(and this pen is going bad now EVERYTHING!!)

And I hate to write in Red! Because red is like . . . well, red is like—anyway, if that's what happenin' like the man says . . .

So, suddenly, instead of mellow we got THIS

       SHIT this issue of

            pumped-up cross SYMBOLIC

              used rebel flag

                  racist pseudo-religious

                    MIND ROT!

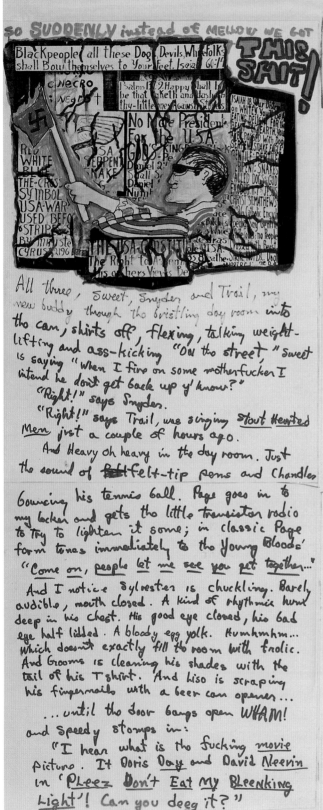

All three, Sweet, Snyder and Trail, my new buddy, though the bristling day room into the can, shirts off, flexing, talking weight-lifting and ass-kicking. "On the street," Sweet is saying "when I fire on some motherfucker I intend he don't get back up y'know?"

"Right!" says Snyder.

"Right!" says Trail, was singing <u>Stout Hearted Men</u> just a couple of hours ago.

And Heavy oh heavy in the day room. Just the sound of ~~felt~~ felt-tip pens and Chandler bouncing his tennis ball. Page goes in to my locker and gets the little transistor radio to try to lighten it some; in classic Page form tunes immediately to the Young Bloods'

"<u>Come on, people let me see you get together...</u>"

And I notice Sylvester is chuckling. Barely audible, mouth closed. A kind of rhythmic hum deep in his chest. His good eye closed, his bad eye half lidded. A bloody egg yolk. Humhmhm... which doesn't exactly fill the room with frolic. And Grooms is cleaning his shades with the tail of his Tshirt. And Liso is scraping his fingernails with a beer can opener...

...until the door bangs open WHAM! and Speedy stomps in:

"I hear what is the fucking <u>movie</u> picture. It <u>Doris Day</u> and David <u>Neevin</u> in '<u>Pleez Don't Eat My Bleenking Light</u>'! Can you <u>deeg</u> it?"

Saturday Morning

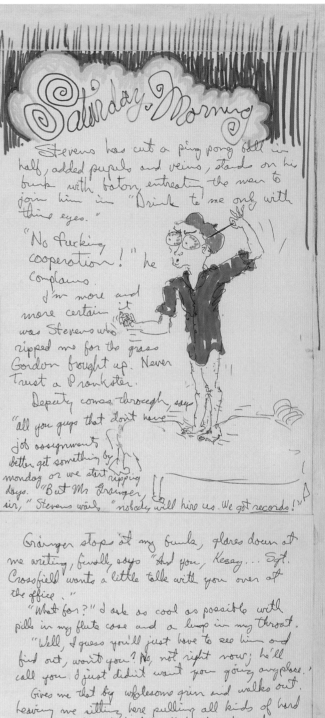

Stevens has cut a ping pong ball in half, added pupils and veins, stands on his bunk with baton, entreating the men to join him in "Drink to me only with thine eyes."

"No fucking cooperation!" he complains.

I'm more and more certain it was Stevens who ripped me for the grass Gordon brought up. Never trust a Prankster.

Deputy comes through, says "all you guys that don't have job assignments better get something by monday or we start ripping days. "But Mr. Grainger sir," Stevens wails "nobody will hire us. We got records!"

Grainger stops at my bunk, glares down at me writing, finally, says "And you, Kesey... Sgt. Crossfield wants a little talk with you over at the office."

"What for?" I ask as cool as possible with pills in my flute case and a lump in my throat.

"Well, I guess you'll just have to see him and find out, won't you? No, not right now; he'll call you. I just didn't want you going anyplace."

Gives me that big wholesome grin and walks out. Leaving me sitting here pulling all kinds of hard time. "I wonder what that's all about," I wonder.

"Maybe nothing," Stevens says. "Maybe just Grainger after your button. I wouldn't worry about it."

So I don't. ~~Foge~~ For about 3 hours. After lunch and inspection I finally decide Grainger was just trying to fuck with my mind and head on down to the pool with the recorder to record some new sides for the

All three—Sweet, Snyder and Trail, my new buddy of the bush—go swaggering through the bristling dayroom into the can, shirts off, flexing, talking weight-lifting and ass-kicking.

"On the street," Sweet is saying, "when I fire on some motherfucker I intend he don't get back up y'know?"

"Right!" says Snyder.

"Right!" says Trail, who was singing "Stout Hearted Men" just a couple of hours ago.

Ah heavy oh heavy in the dayroom. Just the sound of felt-tip pens and Chandler bouncing his tennis ball. Page goes into my locker and gets the little transistor radio to try to lighten it some; in classic Page form he tunes immediately to the Youngbloods singing "Come on people, let me see you get together . . ."

And I notice Sylvester is chuckling. Barely audible, mouth closed. A kind of rhythmic hum deep in chest. His good eye closed, bad eye half-lidded. A bloody egg yolk. Humhmhm . . . which doesn't exactly fill the room with frolic. And Breems is cleaning his thin blue shades with the tail of his T shirt. And Liso is scraping his fingernails with a beer can opener . . .

. . . until the door bangs open WHAM! and Speedy the bantam rooster struts in:

"I hear the fucking movie picture. It Doris Day and David Neevin in 'Pleez Don't Eat My Bleenkin' Light'! Can you deeg it?"

SATURDAY MORNING

Fassenaux has cut a ping pong ball in half, added pupils and veins, stands on his bunk with baton, entreating the men to join him in "Drink to me only with thine eyes."

"No fucking cooperation!" he complains.

I'm more and more certain it was Fassenaux who ripped me for the grass Gordon brought up. Never trust a Prankster.

Deputy comes through says "All you guys that don't have a job assignment better get something by Monday or we start ripping days."

"But Mr. Grainger, sir," Fassenaux wails, "nobody will hire us. We got records!"

Deputy Grainger stops at my bunk, glares down at me writing, finally says "And you, Kesey . . . Sgt. Wayne wants a little talk with you over at the office."

"What for?" I ask as cool as possible with pills in my flute case and a lump in my throat.

"Well, I guess you'll just have to see him and find out, won't you? No, not right now; he'll call you. I just didn't want you going anyplace."

Gives me that big wholesome grin and walks out. Leaving me sitting here pulling all kinds of hard time. "I wonder what's that all about," I wonder out loud.

"Maybe nothing," Fassenaux says. "Maybe just The Duke after your button. I wouldn't worry about it."

So I don't, for about three hours. After lunch and inspection I finally decide Sergeant Wayne was just trying to fuck with my mind and head on down to the pool with the recorder to tape some new sides for the barracks: James has been wearing a little thin. Page is playing KPFA on the FM because there's this Boris Karloff special on with Boris reminiscing about bygone monsters. Lot of bitching by guys wanting music but Page, being a warlock and all, stands on his rights. "We been listening to your fuckin music all <u>fucking morning</u> and now I wanta hear this it's only fair . . ."

And so forth and so on, being <u>reason</u>able as only Page can. So I hook up the recorder and record Boris.

It's sunny and nice. The water sparkling clean since Page has started scrubbing out the algae. A bunch in the pool playing towel tag and romping around. On the sunny side of the pool a bunch of white guys on towels turning slowly in the sun, on the shady side all the Bloods. Beautiful.

Boris is recalling the famous line: "He meddled with things man was meant to leave alone."

"Yeah," Chandler agrees, "Dope."

I don't see Trail anywhere, not sure I want to turn him on anyway after last night. I get into my swimsuit and dive in. I can feel Page sending out his "Well? When are we going to take it?" but I swim around waiting for the signals. Taking acid is pretty jittery business for me under any circumstances. As the trips become less frequent they become wilder. The last time we took it was the solstice, after close to a year without any—and that was such an all-time experience I'm not sure I'm ready again. Especially in jail. But it's so sunny and the trees are so friendly. "And besides," Page reminds me as I walk in to check the tape and get a towel, "nobody's ever been busted for dope they already took."

"Okay. I'll get it. It's in the hem of my shirt." And just as I get the shirt <u>Wham:</u> "KESEY TO THE OFFICE!" over the P.A. "<u>KESEY TO THE OFFICE ON THE DOUBLE!</u>"

I almost shit.

Half dried, half dressed I head up the hill, meet Trail coming down. "They been asking me questions about what you were doing off your work area yesterday." About half-way sarcastic.

"I had a headache and borrowed some aspirin."

"Yeah? Well, the talk is in La Honda you tried to molest some woman."

Tall and rangy, Sergeant Wayne could do a Marlboro Country ad if it wasn't for his eyes. And the Gestapo smile that flashes through his cover now and then.

"Kesey, I think you're due to cause me a lot of trouble. A <u>lot</u> of trouble." Grin. Offers me a cigarette. Tilts back in his chair loving every minute of it. Waits, watching me squirm in his smoke, then fires at me: "Tell me what you did yesterday."

I tell him. It's a good thing Trail tipped me because I'm able to run down my trip across the street in complete open-faced innocence. Which frustrates him so he stops me half-way through: "Didn't it occur to you that you were leaving your work area, technically escaping?"

"No. That occurred to you, not me."

"Why did you do it?"

"I had a headache. I went to the nearest house and borrowed some aspirin."

"Unmindful of the consequences."

"What consequences?"

"Scaring some poor old lady out of her wits."

"Baloney. That old lady? She even wanted me to go back and bring her some kindling."

"Well, the story in La Honda is that Ken Kesey is roaming the woods again scaring the ladies."

"Maybe you better talk with the old lady."

And back and forth and on and on and weirder and weirder. Until it finally begins to come across to me what he wants. Repentance. He's up on some moral pulpit about honor and trust and aspirin being a crutch and I get pissed off and I'm goddamned if I'm about to repent before this Nazi asshole! I can be as self-righteous as he can! Finally I tell him "All right, Sergeant Wayne . . . whatever."

"What?"

"It used to be 'whatever's Right' now it's just 'whatever.' Do whatever you're gonna do. I can dig it."

"Well, first we'll have to investigate . . ." He's thrown off-balance by my sudden surrender.

Psychedelic jiujitsu. "I mean you can kill me but you can't eat me."

"What punishment do you think is just?"

"I don't think any punishment is just."

"You'd just let everybody go, I suppose."

"That's right."

"Murderers and child molesters and lunatics . . ."

"Sergeant, has it occurred to you that no other species has need of cops. Or judges. Or punishment."

"And just who would protect you and your family and children from the murderers and child molesters and lunatics?"

"Who breathes for us when we sleep?"

"Huh?"

That always gets 'em. "Who protects us from the Bogeyman?"

"Wait a minute . . ."

And round and round we go again. An hour later I feel like I've been ravaged by some kinda diabolic psychic sex artist. I stumble out with Wayne's promise that "after Deputy Givens drives up and talks with the woman we'll have another session."

And my head is aching like a bastard and I've missed medication call while I'm in Wayne's office so I don't have any aspirin or Librium and I'm damn sure not interested in LSD. I flop down on my bunk and sleep through supper. But that isn't the problem.

My nest out of tumbleweeds pitched in peaks and snow and air so thin it takes hours, days to weave a call . . . my old man a steel eagle with feathers of pounded brass; my old lady a polar bear. No night or day. Pulsing gray and they take turns foraging the valley, return with sheep and Volkswagens.

My old man would tilt a proud eye and roar, "Someday, m'boy, you'll rank the mother-fuckin <u>moon</u>!"

And mother adds, "<u>Also</u> be the president and the pope and use your <u>spoon</u> on that sheep! Plenty of food, plenty of sleep . . . <u>oh,</u> such fierce and fiery eyes!"

And my old man says, "Exercise! Is what you need. Follow me; see what I treed for you to wrestle."

Some farmer's bull stuck in a bog. Or a rabid motorcycle. Or a mutated hog with wings and 10-penny bristles.

I could sing America before I drew breath, single bound tall buildings with a Jap in my mouth. I was taught to be scared of the fall, not of the death, and that a nigger's a Negro, even down south.

My private tutors were Davy Crockett, Abe Lincoln and John Wayne. My coaches Tarzan and Ford and Alley Oop. I dated Monroe and Bergman and the jet-propelled plane. And drunk moonshine and Coke and LSD soup.

I was reared by a world made of tears and concrete. I'm strong by millions and ready to start scraping the shit from the yellow brick road, ready to pull the motor out of the rust. I'm strong by centuries of "Be free. Be kind. Be just." I'm strong by bleeding the weaker man's pain. I'm strong by seeing my own weaknesses plain. I'm strong by millions and ready for my work.

I wait but for the go-ahead from the Folks . . . who have been frightened by their offspring . . . who have lost faith in their heart's creation . . . who can't believe their American Dream.

"Bless me, Folks! I'm smoking and churning the tracks. Bless me free, Folks, or damnit turn off the steam!" Instead, somebody shakes me awake in the dark. "Here you go, Keys. I thought you might like a little snack . . ."

Jesus Christ! It's Szikso. With a <u>huge</u> steak sandwich. And a glass of real milk!

SUNDAY MORN AND it's sunny again. I get some more India ink. Nice music, everybody in their Sunday best. Page comes over slicked and grinning. So okay. Let's get high.

Jiggedy Jog Jiggedy Jog, **drop** a **cap** & **slip** a **cog.**

Everybody jams up in C Barracks overlooking the parking lot to check the cars coming scope the people. Trail's wife always first. "I get her to be parked at the gate a half hour before it opens so we can take <u>our table</u>."

Best. Page comes over slicked and grinning. So okay. Let's get high.

Jiggedy Jog. Jigged Jog, drop a cap & slip a cog.

Everybody jams up in C barracks overlooking parking lot check the cars coming scope the people. Trail's wife always first. ("I get her to be parked at the gate a half hour before it opens. So we can get our table.") Then Henry's succulent Polynesian wife and her succulent sister who has to wait in the car right at the bottom of C barracks back steps, tempting and lush by the window. Oh me.

C'mon now! You know it's to early to

FFS FAR STING

Concentrate Concentrate Concentrate! CONCENTRATE! long lack of contact and bam! "GURLS!" the image vibrate wait

then "KESEY...DROWNING..." to the visiting area Tease!"

THE HERE

A whole shitload! Chuck and sue and Bud & sherry and Paula Fry & Jenny (the two "cousins") and all the kids and fried chicken and Coca Cola and pie and they're all loaded too. BUZZZ goes the visiting area. Much food. Much color much laughing and quick Click

of look we've loaded in foil and glowing and buzzing like a hive of Neon Bees!

Over there's Zorro with his patch on and his lovely platinum blond, her hair piled to the sky, and over there's Goldie and her newborn baby super-wired, and over there's Trail with his wife at there special table. And the trees applaud the whole crew.

BUT — back at the ranch

Grooms scoping down on Henry's wife "Mmm. MMM!" he purrs. "If she aint foxy then I just do not know!" He loads his pipe. "What she needs is to light some dudes pipe."

Liso: "That off-limits..."

Grooms: "Where off-limits. You show me a sign off-limits."

Liso, pointing out sign on C barracks back porch "O-F-F limits."

Grooms: "Oh... that off limits."

was how liso told it

"Next thing I know"

"there's Grooms hunkered down at the car window, rapping to Henry's wife's succulent sister a mile a minute, off limits be damned. Get on, Grooms!"

A double good afternoon. Marred only by Smathers being called up from the visiting area by Grainger (apparently was getting too cozy with his woman for Grainger's comfort) and by the news that Chocolate George has been snuffed by some hit-&-run in the city. We don't give Smather's problem much thought, and Chocolate's death is sad but, like Mountain Girl says, "It doesn't have to be heavy just because it's sad."

Then Henry's succulent Polynesian wife and her succulent sister who has to wait in her car right at the bottom of C Barracks' back steps, tempting and lush by the window. Oh me. C'mon now! You know it's too early to fee

eeee

EEEE

EEL

ANYTHINGWait!

concentrate,   concentrate, concentrate!

CONCENTRATE long lack of contact and bam!

"GURLS!" The image vibrates wait . . . wait . . .

then "Kesey . . . BROWNING . . . to the visiting area please." THEY HERE!

PEOPLE   A whole shit load! Chuck and Sue and Bud and Sherry and M.G. and Paula Fry and Jenny (the two "cousins") and all the kids and fried chicken and Coca-Cola and pie and they're all loaded too **BUZZZzzzzzzzz**zzzzzzzzzzzzzzzzzzz goes the visiting area. Much food. Much color. Much laughing and quick click of <u>look</u> we're loaded in jail and glowing and buzzing like a hive of <u>Neon Bees</u>!

Over there is Zorro with his Hell's Angel rocker patch on and his lovely platinum blond Angel Mama, her hair piled to the sky . . . and over there's Goldie and his newborn baby super-wired, and over there's Trail with his wife at their special table. And the trees applaud the whole crew.

BUT back at the porch in the forlorn collection of inmates that didn't get visitors is Breems and he is way too uncool how he's scoping down on Henry's wife's sister so obvious. "Mmm. MMM!" he purrs. "If she ain't foxy then I just do not <u>know</u>!" He loads his Sherlock Holmes meerschaum. "What she needs is to light some dude's <u>pipe</u>!"

LISO: "That off-limits, Home . . . "

BREEMS: "Where off-limits? You show me a sign anywhere say off-limits."

LISO, pointing out a sign on C Barracks back porch: "O-F-F Limits."

BREEMS: "Oh <u>that</u> off-limits."

"Next thing I know," was how Liso told it later, "there's Breems hunkered down at the car window, rapping to Henry's wife's succulent <u>sister</u> a mile a minute, off-limits be damned hee hee. Get on, <u>Breems</u>!"

A double-good afternoon, though. Marred only by Smuthers being called up from the visiting area by Sergeant Wayne (apparently he was getting too cozy with his women for Wayne's comfort), and by the news that Chocolate George had been snuffed by some hit-and-run in the city. We don't give Smuthers' problems much thought, and Chocolate's death is sad but, like Mountain Girl says, "It doesn't have to be heavy just because it's sad."

So after visit Page & I go to the Chapel and flute and strum a wordless eulogy to a friend...

CHOCOLATE GEORGE HAS GONE WHERE ALL GOOD ANGELS GO GO AHEAD ON GEORGE

myself swept up in a cathartic ritual, exorcizing some ~~grim~~ gnawing demon by butting heads with fellows plagued by the same demon. Taking on somebody innocent of the demon's tooth is a lopsided battle, locking spice in a grim glitter says: "I gonna blow, I'm packed so teeth-gritting full, & gonna let loose and blow... anybody feel like they're up to blowing with me?"

And Sylvester, breathing hard, dusty purple gasping volcanoe -- says, laughing, "Give it to me and I run the motherfucker around end!" Thud. He means full out. I can dig it. Thud.

FULL OUT followed by **THUD** Bone jar ringing those little ~~at~~ earlier at the edge of my eyes. "Let me run it again." Chug **HUGGGUG!** Touchdown! Then the other team scores. The playing gets fiercer, loosser. Bloodier. ~~More on~~ Moove on end-around, hip with flag in pocket next to fence. I got to get my face in there to stop him, scrape the hide off my arm. I can dig it.

I hear Trail yelling up there. Don't know who for.

We win. Sylvester chugging right up the middle and me blocking just like I'm in shape.

Lots of Bloods grouped griping about something outside of office. I pick up something about Grainger, to do with his turning away some Negro visitors of dubious ID, and his calling Smithers to the office. Pulsing, hornet-nest hum around the whole area. Goldie shows up with a football. Let's get up a game!"

Lower area, Sundowning, Page and I the only white guys want to play. Chose up side. Lots of yelling, lots of juice buzzing round. Hillside above the field thick with spectators. I holler at Trail: "Come on down and play." No thanks...

Kick off. Sylvester gathers it up and I block. Thud. Not exactly tackle because we got flags, but close, close... Dust in your nose. Thud. This aint no half-way game, this is a game with knife in pockets. Thud. We begin to groove. The Bloods sense Page and I are jacked up past caring about broken bones, bloody noses and that's the way they like it. I feel

Everybody else wants to go another touchdown. Or til its to dark to play. But I'm finished. I get Page's keys and stroll down to the pool.

The water is still. The circle of redwood spires reflected in the surface. Open Page's shack and put on Kyto and flute. Wish I had a clean change of clothes, not these sweaty and dusty rags. I dive in naked, without taking the mandatory shower, splash... glide with my eyes closed, body straight. Head for tuned with jewels & whirligigs & skyrockets. Glide long as I can. Surface into Kyto & Flute. And Trail standing at the pool's edge. We look at each other. Until I say "I thought you were gonna push iron with Sweet & Snyder."

So after visit Page and I go to the chapel and flute and strum a wordless eulogy to a friend . . . Chocolate George has gone where all Good Angels go. Go ahead on, George . . .

Lots of Bloods grouped griping about something outside the office. I pick up something about Sergeant Wayne, to do with his turning away some Negro visitors of dubious ID, and his calling Smuthers to the office. Pulsing, hornet-nest hum around the whole area. Goldie shows up with a football. "Let's get up a game!"

Perfect.

Lower area, sunsdowning, Page and I the only white guys want to play. Choose up sides. Lots of yelling, lots of juice buzzing round. Hillside above the field thick with spectators. I holler at Trail: "Come on down and play." No thanks.

Kickoff. Sylvester gathers it up and I block. Thud. Not exactly tackle because we got flags. But close, close . . . Dust in your nose. Thud. This ain't no half-way game, I perceive. This is a game with knives like demon teeth in pockets of the mind. Thud. We begin to Groove. The Bloods sense Page and I are jacked up past caring about broken bones, bloody noses, and that's the way they like it. I feel myself swept up in a cathartic ritual, exorcising some gnawing demon by butting heads with fellows plagued by the same demon. Taking on somebody innocent of the demon's tooth is a lopsided battle, lacking spice— so I put on grim glitter face that says: "I gonna <u>blow</u>. I'm packed so teeth-gritting full, I gotta let loose and <u>blow</u> . . . anybody feel like they're up to blowing with me?"

And Sylvester—breathing hard, dusty purple gasping volcano—asks, laughing, "Kesey, can you pull and block?"

"Like a motherfucker."

"Then lead block me around the motherfucker end!"

Thud. He means full out I can dig it. Thud.

FULL

OUT

followed by a

THUD bone jar ringing those little curlicues on the edge of my eyes. "Lead me—run it again!" Chug CHUG **CHUG**! Touchdown! Then the other team scores. The playing gets fiercer, looser. Bloodier. Moore on end-around, hip with flag in pocket next to fence. I got to get my face in there to stop him, scrape the hide off my arm. I can dig it.

I hear Trail yelling up there. Don't know who for.

We win. Sylvester chugging right up the middle and me blocking just like I'm back in varsity shape. Everybody else wants to go to another touchdown. Or till it's too dark to play. But I'm finished. I get Page's keys and stroll down to the pool.

The water is still. The circle of redwood spires reflected in the surface. Open Page's shack and put on koto and flute. Wish I had a clean change of clothes, not these sweaty and dusty rags. I dive in naked without taking the mandatory shower, splash . . . going with my eyes closed, body straight. Head fortuned with jewels & whirligigs & skyrockets. Glide long as I can. Surface into koto and flute. And Trail standing at the pool's edge. We look at each other. Until I say

"I thought you were going to push iron with Sweet and Snyder."

"Maybe after supper." Begins combing his hair. "So those were what do you call them? The Pranksters?"

"A few of them."

"I hear those girls are the cousins that brought up your flute."

"Right." I start drying myself.

"Good-looking pieces. In fact, they were all good-looking people."

He says this sincerely, then simply: "You'd be surprised if I told you who my people are."

I go into the shack. "Trail. There's a little bit of tape I want you to hear . . ." I put the earphones to him, zoom the tape to Boris Karloff reminiscing about lycanthropy . . .

> <u>Even a man who is pure in heart</u>
> <u>And says his prayers at night</u>
> <u>May turn to a wolf when the wolfbane blooms</u>
> <u>And the moon is full and bright</u>

Then about the old Gypsy Lady in "<u>The Wolfman</u>" and her strange chant over the dead form of the ill-fated Larry Talbot, finally felled by silver in his heart: "<u>It is through no fault of your own that your walk was funny, my son—</u>"

That ancient, eerie voice twines from the shabby speakers out into the dusk; Trail presses the earphones tight with both hands, eyes round and unbelieving.

"<u>—but even as the sparks fly upward to heaven and the rivers flow down to the sea . . . so, too, tears shall reach their predestined end.</u>"

Trail snatches the phones from his head like they were hot: "Motherfuck!"—overwhelmed that anyone could penetrate his hustle; awestruck by the neat little cosmic coincidences of just that phrase on tape. "Mother<u>fuck</u>! That hit the nail right on the motherfucking <u>head</u>!"

I can hear the Blood-pack on their way to the pool. And the high sharp mosquito whine of the sewage plant.

Now About a Group . . .

"Some people sleep been workin all day you layin around on your motherfuckin ass—"
(THE IMPORTANT THING IS DISTURB A LITTLE SHIT SEE)

"—playing

like kids."

"Kids? I ain't playin no kids. I got fo' kids and I don't even play wif dem!"

The important thing is you keep 'em stirred up amongst each other, see? (this is top secret, you understand) and that way they don't turn on the <u>establishment</u> (which works both ways, of course).

But you got to be careful not to let it get out of hand where you're forced to step in and lower the boom . . . because that could cause them to turn on you! (unpredictable mother-fuckers) IF YOU ARE THE HEAT YOU GOT TO BE CAREFUL. THE FLAMES ARE

RIGHT
HERE

SOMEWHERE.

My head still aches from that tree. And I'm tired listening to the same old wrang-ling . . .

Then we're into a hassle between Smuthers and Sergeant Wayne about visiting day:

"You got no right callin' me down in front of my folks and such, all the way across the visiting area . . . "

"Listen, Smuthers, we say no hanky-panky and that means under the table as well as on top . . . "

"Yeah, well," Smuthers muttering, "there's <u>some</u> here . . . "

Focus on Trail. Everybody knows about Trail's wife, gets there first on Sunday, a hole in her tights at the crotch. And everybody knows that Sergeant Wayne is fond of Trail. And, yeah, why ain't <u>Trail</u> ever called down?

"Yeah . . . yeah . . . yeah . . . " Sick Blood mutter that ain't scaring Wayne none at all. But this is <u>Blood Business happening</u>! Uh oh . . . could turn dangerous. Quick then! Shift someplace else! Talk about socks. Or about guys running to the mess hall. Or about poli-tics, hip-square, left-right, or about "Restrooms to be used after hours for natural causes only"—about anything but DON'T TALK ABOUT BLACK-WHITE! (specially if you're a deputy in a work camp with a bunch of black and white thugs and help a good hour away).

So back into wrangling on the levels of lesser heat. When we gonna get clean socks? Who's stole Talley's lock? When you gonna fix the TV? Because a cop is usually a peace-loving dove down deep. Acts tough because he's scared of the higher-up hawks he works for.

SNARL

GROWL

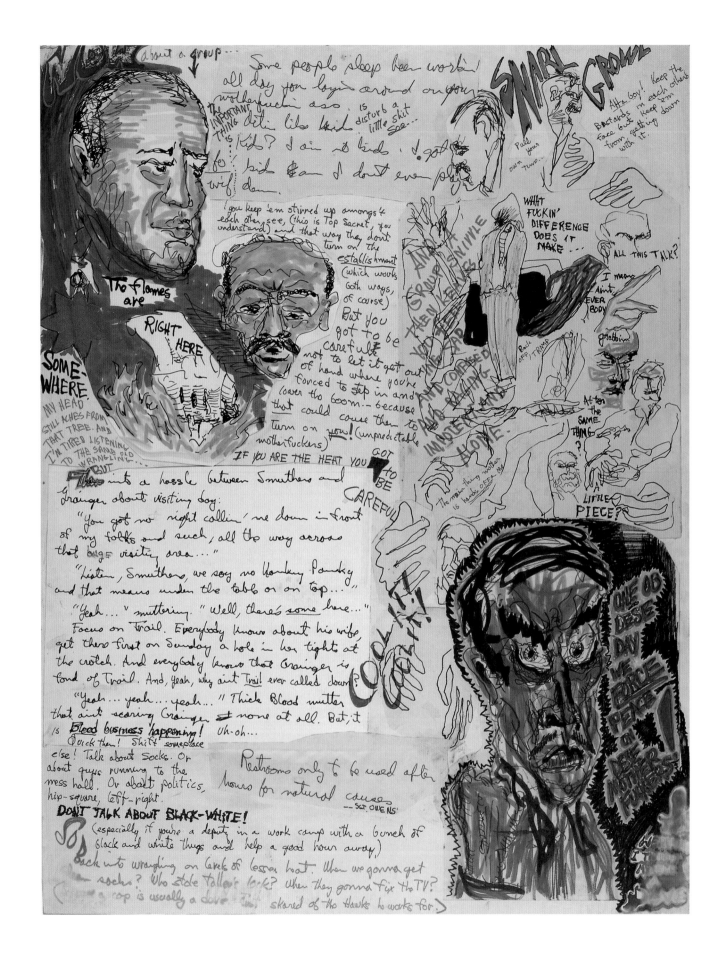

LOOK about a group...

Some people sleep been workin' all day you loyin' around on your motherfuckin' ass. The IMPORTANT THING deth like kids is disturb a little shit see...

Kid? I ain't kids. I got fo' kid an I don't even play wif dem.

(You keep 'em stirred up amongs't each other, see, (this is Top Secret, you understand) and that way they don't turn on the establishment (which works both ways, of course) But you got to be careful not to let it get out of hand where you're forced to step in and lower the boom -- because that could cause them to turn on you! (unpredictable motherfuckers)

IF YOU ARE THE HEAT YOU GOT TO BE CAREFUL

The flames are RIGHT HERE

SOMEWHERE. MY HEAD STILL ACHES FROM THAT TREE. AND I'M TIRED LISTENING TO THE SAME OLD WRANGLING... BUT

SNARL GROWL

Atta boy! Keep the bastards in each others face but keep 'em from gettin' with it.

Pull your own two...

AND A GROUP SNIVLE THEN LEADERS AND CONFUSED AND RAILING IMPOTENTLY ALONE.

WHAT FUCKIN' DIFFERENCE DOES IT MAKE...

ALL THIS TALK?

I mean. I Aint EVER BODY grabbin'...

Back OFF, TRAMP

At ten the SAME THING?

A LITTLE PIECE?

The main thing matter is hands OFF A ME

This into a hassle between Smothers and Grainger about visiting boy:

"You got no right callin' me down in front of my folks and such, all the way across that large visiting area..."

"Listen, Smothers, we say no hanky panky and that means under the tabb or on top..."

"Yeah..." muttering. "Well, there's some here..."

Focus on Trail. Everybody knows about his wife, get there first on Sunday a hole in her tights at the crotch. And everybody knows that Grainger is fond of Trail. And, yeah, why aint Trail ever called down?

"Yeah... yeah... yeah..." Thick Blood mutter that aint scaring Grainger none at all. But, it is Blood business happening! Uh-oh...

Quick then! Shift someplace else! Talk about Socks. Or about guys running to the mess hall. Or about politics, hip-square, left-right.

COOL IT! COOL IT!

Restrooms only to be used after hours for natural causes -- SGT. OWENS

ONE OB DESSE DAY WE FORCE PEACE ON DESE MOTHER FUKERS

DON'T TALK ABOUT BLACK-WHITE!
(especially if you're a deputy in a work camp with a bunch of black and white thugs and help a good hour away.)

Back into wrangling on levels of lesser heat. When we gonna get socks? Who stole Taller's fork? When they gonna fix the TV? (a cop is usually a dove that scared of the Hawks he works for.)

Atta boy! Keep the bastards in each other's face but keep 'em from getting down and dirty with it.

<u>COOL IT!</u>

<u>COOL IT!</u>

What fuckin' difference does it make ... all this talk? A good group snivel leaves you feeling sad and confused and raging impotent and alone. The main thing Mother is <u>hands offa</u> me! I mean ain't ever body grabbin after the same thing? A little piece? ONE OB DESE DAY WE

FORCE

PEACE ON DESE MOTHERFUCKERS!

"WHO'S?

that sniffing at my door?"

cried the fair young sex fiend.

The door was locked and fettered and buttered to her taste. The moon outside her window full and teasing to her chaste white body. Sniff snof, continued still ... **UNTIL**

... at that instant the cock crowed the cat mewed and a ghost fled, complaining of severe pains in his back and head. Dreams dream on.

GROUP MONDAY NIGHT

Giggling buncha apes, already sentenced ... found guilty and sentenced. Therefore somehow innocent ... Laugh at a fart or a belch, make nasty kissing sounds in each other's ear: "Big HAIRY LIPS on that motherfucker."

"Don't rank it fellas," says Fassenaux. "We're just sitting here sweat popping off our brother's brow."

Do Unto The Other Mother

Before The Other Mother

Do Unto You.

Adams says "You know when I'm on the street I sleep in a coffin?"

"Horseshit," Fassenaux says.

"Smell me," Adams says. "Ain't I a flower?"

Boom BLOOM **BLOOM** <u>**BLOOM**</u> meeting come to order.

Adams still fairly new asks "Hey, you want honesty? Alright I want to know how come they got all these groovy groups come to the aid of alkies while nothing for us poor dope fiends?"

Harrison the county-paid do-good supposed to take care of such business answers all serious, "Now there have been plans—still on the small scale of course—to deal with the problem of drugs. How<u>ever</u>—"

However and so forth and blah, blah, blah—hand moving in a mechanical gesture for clumsy emphasis ... mouth going up and down and when he finishes talking everybody's

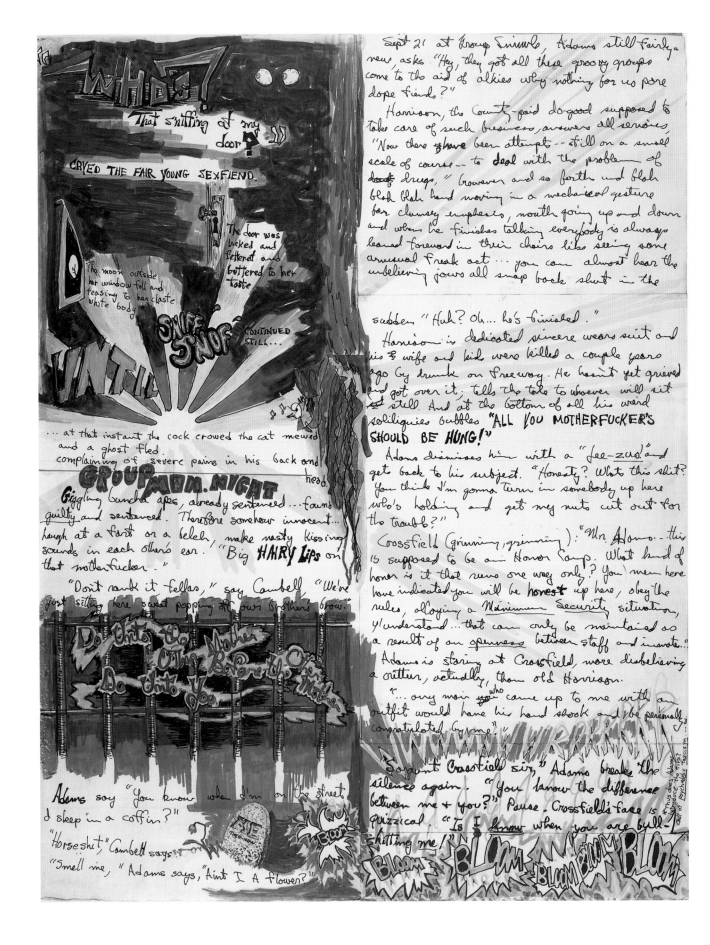

always leaned forward in their chairs like seeing some unnatural freak act. Then you can almost hear the unbelieving jaws all snap back shut in a sudden "Huh? OH . . . he's finished."

Harrison is dedicated sincere wears suits and his wife and kids were killed a couple years ago by a drunk on the freeway. He hasn't yet grieved and got over it. Tells the tale to whoever will sit still for his prolonged sorrowful song. But at the bottom of all his weird soliloquies always bubbles the unvoiced roar: "ALL YOU MOTHERFUCKERS SHOULD BE HUNG!"

Adams dismisses him with a "Jee-zus!" and gets back to the subject. "Honesty? What's this shit? You think I'm going to turn in somebody up here who's holding and get my nuts cut out for my trouble?"

Crossfield (grinning, grinning): "Mr. Adams . . . this is supposed to be an honor camp. What kind of honor is it that runs one way only? You men here have indicated you will be honest up here, obey the rules allowing a <u>minimum security situation</u>, y'under-stand . . . that can only be maintained as a result of an <u>openness</u> between staff and inmates."

Adams is staring at Crossfield, more disbelievable a critter, actually, than old Harrison. "Hey any man who come up to me with an outfit would have his hand shook and be personally congratulated by me."

Shocked gasping, the fan going wwwWWHIRRRrrr.

"Sergeant Crossfield sir," Adams breaks the silence again. "You know the difference between me and you—?"

Pause. Crossfield's face is quizzical.

"—is I <u>know</u> when you are bullshitting <u>me</u>!"

—BLOOM **BLOOM**

BLOOM BLOOM BOOM BOOM—

TERRIFIC RIFF RAP OF YELPING

<u>RAP</u> RAP rap **RAP**

rap **RAP RAP** activity!

After Adams' shot at Crossfield the meeting picks up. Crossfield's a little stunned with paranoia ("<u>Do they know something I don't?</u>")—communicates it to the rest of the staff. All the deputies checking each other across the circle to make sure they aren't alone.

Fassenaux shoots one in while Crossfield struggles for cleanup. "What Adams here is <u>saying</u>, Mister Crossfield, is right now alla us can see in your face you got your covers pulled."

I follow up with, "But you don't have the same perception." Black fiery eyes at me: "And how do you know <u>that</u>, Mr. Kesey?"

"Because if you were able to see into us that way then you wouldn't be after us to be your camp sleuths, right?"

Then Sergeant Wayne says something to me that stops our rally cold—like calling

TEREBIFFIC RAP YELPING ACTIVITY

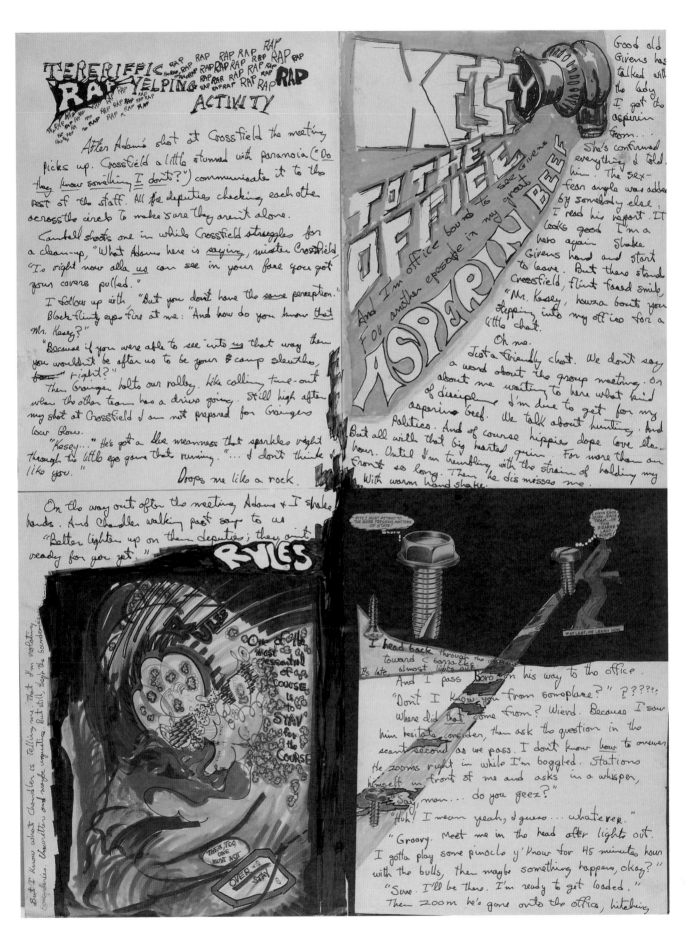

After Adam's shot at Crossfield the meeting picks up. Crossfield a little stunned with paranoia ("Do they know something I don't?") communicates it to the rest of the staff. All the deputies checking each other across the circle to make sure they aren't alone.

Cantrell shoots one in while Crossfield struggles for a clean-up, "What Adams here is saying, mister Crossfield, is right now alla us can see in your face you got your covers pulled."

I follow up with, "But you don't have the same perception." Black flinty eyes fire at me: "And how do you know that Mr. Kesey?"

"Because if you were able to see into us that way then you wouldn't be after us to be your & camp sleuths, right?"

Then Grainger halts our rally. Like calling time-out when the other team has a drive going. Still high after my shot at Crossfield I am not prepared for Grainger's low blow.

"Kesey..." He's got a blue meanness that sparkles right through his little eyes game that running. "... I don't think I like you."

Drops me like a rock.

On the way out after the meeting Adams & I shake hands. And Chandler walking past says to us "Better lighten up on them deputies; they ain't ready for you yet."

KEY TO THE OFFICE ASPIRIN BEEF

And I'm office bound to see Givens for another episode in my great ASPIRIN BEEF

Good old Givens has talked with the lady I got the aspirin from... She's confirmed everything I told him. The sex-fear angle was added by somebody else. I read his report. It looks good I'm a hero again. Shake Givens hand and start to leave. But there stands Crossfield, flint faced smile, "Mr. Kesey, howza bouts you stepping into my office for a little chat.

Oh me.

Just a friendly chat. We don't say a word about the group meeting. Or me waiting to hear what kind of discipline I'm due to get for my aspirin beef. We talk about hunting. And Politics. And of course hippie dope love etc.. But all with that big hearted grin. For more than an hour. Until I'm trembling with the strain of holding my front so long. Then he dismisses me. With warm hand shake.

RULES

One of the most essential of aa course is to STAY for the COURSE

THEN TOO ONE MUST NOT OVER STAY

But I know what Chandler is telling me. That I'm violating conventions. Unwritten and maybe unjust is. But still, though the boredness

FITY I MUST ATTEND TO THE MORE PRESSING MATTERS OF STATE.

KNOW EACH QUIRK—BACK OF THIS TRAP—OF THIS BIZARRE LAND SCAPE!

WAIT, LAST, WE LEARN HOW

I head back through the toward Gorge. It's late, almost lights out. And I pass Boro on his way to the office.

"Don't I know you from someplace?" ?????

Where did that come from? Wierd. Because I saw him hesitate consider, then ask the question in the scant second as we pass. I don't know how to answer. He zooms right in while I'm boggled. Stations himself in front of me and asks in a whisper, "Say, man... do you geez?"

"Huh! I mean yeah, I guess ... whatever."

"Groovy. Meet me in the head after lights out. I gotta play some pinoclo y'know for 45 minutes hour with the bulls, then maybe something happens, okay?"

"Sure. I'll be there. I'm ready to get loaded."

Then zoom he's gone onto the office, hitching

time-out when the other team has a drive going. I'm all adrenaline pumped after my shot across Crossfield's bow, and not prepared for Wayne's low blow:

"Kesey—?" He's got a blue meanness that sparkles right through the little ego game that's been taking place. "I don't think I like you."

Just beneath the waterline . . . sinks me like a stone. I don't make another peep the whole damn meeting.

On the way out after the meeting Adams and I shake hands. And Chandler walking by says to us, "Better lighten up on them deputies; they ain't ready for you yet." He's a sweetheart, Chandler is . . . reminding me in his own loose-lipped way of the **UNWRIT RULES.**

Rule 1 and one of the most essential of course if one wants to stay for the course, is: "One Must Not Overstay."

Chandler in his loose-grin way is warning me and Adams that we are violating boundaries, barely visible and surely unjust. But still, they're boundaries . . . just as the multi-throated camp sound system bellers **KESEY**

TO THE

OFFICE!

About face and I'm office bound to see Givens for another episode in the ongoing saga of my great ASPIRIN BEEF.

Good old Givens, more counselor than cop, he's actually driven down and talked with the lady I got the aspirin from. She's confirmed everything I told Wayne. The sex-fear angle was added by somebody else. I read his report. It looks good. I'm a hero again. Shake Givens' hand and start to leave. But there stands Crossfield, flint-face smile:

"Mr. Kesey, howzabout stepping into <u>my</u> office for a little chat."

Oh me.

Just a friendly chat. We don't say a word about the group meeting. Or about me waiting to hear what kind of discipline I'm due to get over the aspirin beef. We talk about hunting. And politics. And of course hippies dope love etc. But all with a big-hearted grin. For more than an hour. Then he dismisses me. With a warm handshake.

I head back through the ice plants toward C Barracks. It's late, almost lights out. And I pass Szikso on his way to the office.

"Don't I know you from someplace?" he asks in a whisper absolutely oozing with wickedness. Where did <u>that</u> come from? Weird. Because I saw him hesitate, consider, then ask the question in the scant second as we pass. I don't know how to answer. He zooms right in while I'm boggled. Stations himself in front of me and asks in a whisper, "Say man . . . do you geez?"

"Huh! I mean yeah, I guess . . . whatever."

"Groovy. Meet in the head after lights out. I gotta play some pinochle and gossip with the bulls y'know for 45 minutes or an hour, then maybe something happens, okay?"

I've had a lot of guys caution me about Szikso and his little cards-and-gossip get-togethers. But like a dedicated fool I answer "Sure, why not . . . I'm ready to get loaded."

Then zoom he's gone into the office, hitching his britches like Jimmy Cagney in *Public Enemy Number One,* leaving me standing scratching my belly. Motherfuckin <u>weird</u> is all there is to it. But I could use a little crystal, stay up all night, write a bunch of letters and shit. And maybe Szikso could use a friend. Nobody else has too much to do with him now I think about it. Sure, Szikso, whatever . . .

Dayroom. Nearly midnight. I got the tape machine out here but it's too late to turn on the speakers. I fiddle around sketching, listen to *Sergeant Pepper* twice through the earphones then give them to Chandler and go get into the nightgown Faye made for me. It's a long flannel red-and-white striped affair that Santa Claus might wear. It caused such a laugh when it came in the mail that I had to wear it. It still prompts sniggers and comments even in the dark dorm. I give them a big stretch and yawn. I'm relieved that Szikso didn't show.

Chandler is still bopping around the dayroom, eyes closed and the earphones so loud I can make out the song: "—<u>I</u> get by with a little help from my friends." I wash my face and brush my all-American tooth and head back through the dayroom and take one last look out the screen door and sure enough right on cue here comes Szikso from his card game. He doesn't speak, goes right on in the head. I stroll in after him.

"Listen, Keez,"—immediately in my face, earnest and intimate, his hand on my elbow, "I got the stuff but I couldn't get an outfit nowhere."

Waits. Oh, it's a question. "I don't have one."

He's surprised. "I thought you said you geezed stuff?" Accusing me of not being completely straight with him.

"I've shot stuff a couple of times but that's all. I damn sure don't have a fit . . ."

"Shit. Well, I know this other guy we can borrow from. But that means we have to split this dime paper three ways. There might not be enough to get off on. How much it take for you, good morphine?"

"Morphine? I thought you were talking about speed."

He's surprised again. "Don't you do smack?"

"No. Never have, but I'm always willing to try whatever the Good Lord or the Devil sets in front of me."

"Groovy, man, just let me talk to this other dude."

We go back to the dayroom. Chandler's cherubic face bobbing around in the earphones. Szikso goes to him and removes the earphones, whispers something and the two of them duck into the head. This time I'm surprised; Chandler's always looked too goofy and innocent to be a guy with a fit stashed. But then again, maybe that's why he always looks goofy and innocent. And that's why Henry and Zorro and some of the other hard dudes are so tight with the beardless, limp-grinned flower child. Maybe it isn't sex at all.

They come back out. Szikso heads off back outside, bustling and important. Chandler comes toward me, no trace of the happy face that was bouncing between the earphones a moment before.

"Listen . . . what do you know about this thing with Szikso?"

"Nothing. Probably just what you know."

"He wanted to borrow my outfit, and shit I mean Szikso? So I told him no, then he said you were in on it and wanted to use it and all of a sudden I started getting <u>paranoid</u>, man, like <u>weird</u> paranoid."

Click. There in front of me. "By God, Chandler, you're right! I knew there was something funny about it but I just thought it was Szikso. You're <u>right</u>; I felt it too but I didn't believe it. Don't loan it to him."

"Yeah." Chandler was visibly trembling now. "Yeah, when he comes back I'll tell him when I looked my fit was gone, my stash busted. Weird . . ."

"Ain't it. Listen, I'm going to bed and think about a lot of stuff."

"Boy, I never been hit so hard with paranoia."

A TANK AGAIN

JUST US SITTIN AROUND THE DAYROOM after breakfast before call to board the work bus—and

"Mister Kesey to the office."

"Kesey gonna sweep the competition this week for the Most Popular man in jail," Fassenaux tells me when I leave.

It was Crossfield again <u>asking</u> me about my head. "Feels fair. I'm going out on the job."

"You sure you shouldn't see the doctor?" Now what? I'm confused as shit. Is he really concerned? Is it just a trap? Zap! I'm alert. "No . . . I don't think so . . ."

I see Bushie across the office, giving me a weird look. I come on to Crossfield a minute about "You've either got to <u>let</u> me make those kind of decisions—like letting me know when to get my aspirin—or make my decisions <u>for me</u>! Just let me know which way you want it."

"Now, Ken, you aren't being exactly <u>fair</u> . . ."

"My headache's stopped. I'm waiting for the bus."

"Maybe you'd better get some x-rays. Weren't you hit right where that train hit you?"

Christ, how did he know about <u>that</u>? Sergeant Wayne sitting there scrowling, adds "Yeah, we don't want you accusing us of some old scar. If Sergeant Crossfield thinks it's a good idea to get x-rays then I'd fucking <u>go</u>!"

<u>Ah-hah</u>! Wayne's <u>so</u> obvious. "You guys are scared I'll sue you!" I'm delighted. I've pinned them. Crossfield is shook. Bushie's a little shamefaced. He knows Wayne would like an excuse to wring my simpering neck. "You guys talk about <u>honor</u> and <u>honesty</u> and <u>trust</u>. Does that just mean for the <u>other</u> side? Don't you know that you'll never get more from us than you give? Don't you know that we won't respect the law until it respects us?"

And that asshole Wayne breaks into that big come-on-try-me-punk grin and says, "Kesey . . . you know what your trouble is? You ain't realistic."

So here I sit, contemplating truth and watching Sylvester clean the shitter. Both of us waiting for Deputy Rhack to take us down to the jail in Redwood to see this nutty old doctor. Sylvester scheduled to see him about his bad eye, and me, my head.

    Oh thick and fast
    Thick and fast
    They clock each other running past
    And wave the winners with a flag of truce
    Cut the motherfuckers loose.

DEPUTY RHACK?

(of historical note he came into my life CRASH gun-first through my bathroom window La Honda where Page is standing in the bathtub shaving while Lee Quarn-strom's at the door rapping, and me, depending on which story you buy, I am either (1) flushing grass down the toilet or (2) painting flowers on the toilet or (3) engaging in some even more heinous act as yet uncharged and un-denied.

CRASH! there's this unknown Oriental on my back whacking at me with his flashlight. He turns out to be the sinister arch-agent, Willy Wong. At the bathroom window there's this exhilarated face on the end of a turkey neck and this turkey turns out to be Deputy Rhack, one of the 17 deputies and feds and dogs and police women who busted us at La Honda three years ago. Now he's driving me down to county jail to get my head x-rayed because a tree happened to hit me same place a train did not to mention Willy Wong's flashlight. Small world after all. Wong is whacking me in deepening despair because he can see the pound of grass he and his henchman planted on us by hiding it in a quart fruit jar in the La Honda creekhouse where we would be sure to find it so Willy and his nark-pack could be sure of finding it, too, when they swoop in for the bust but I was too fast for 'em I'd been suspicious about that fruit jar fulla weed from outta nowhere and when Hagen rushes in and shouts "There's cops Everywhere!" I had that jar in a flash and was flushing it before the fuzz could even yell Open Up in the name of the LAW! By the time Willy made it into the crapper the Evil Weed was swirling down down and away and all he could do was whack me fecklessly with his flashlight and keep on whacking until Babbs rushes in and snatches him off my back by the collar, Wong sailing back knocking Page over in the bathtub then jumps back up and goes to whacking at Babbs whack whack whack until Babbs tells him "Stop that!" and Wong stops. Amazed. Then abashed. Then pissed. Then turns to Page sitting baffled and lathered in the tub and charges him with resisting arrest. That charge is the reason Page is doing the time with me and not any of the dozen others who were also in the house. Interesting . . .)

Paste here if I ever find the trial picture of Rhack on top of bus took night of La Honda bust, standing up there holding his flashlight and grinning like he was demented Prometheus and on back of photo autographed "Deputy J. Rhack."

Now he is the transportation officer at the camp, makes daily runs with guys to see the doctor, lawyer, probation officers down in Redwood.

DRIVE BACK through AMERICA

> You've been a couple months
>
> truly separated from the El Camino of USA
>
> And you see it sudden again— <u>Wheeeeee!</u>

Five of us booked to ride into town with Rhack. Standing around the camp office while he shows off his latest prize. Big-time high-rent rifle he ordered from Sweden or someplace. Remind me of something Bushie said once out on the job. I put it in a letter to Faye:

Lunchbreak in the Bush with Bushie. Telling the crew about the time he had left in his pickup a cap gun from his square dance club and got grouped for it.

"What's a work supervisor doing with a gun?"

"Well Rhack always carries a gun with him," Bushie replies.

"Yeah but with Rhack that's different."

I seen they were right. With Rhack that's his security blanket. Take his gun away from him, he'd have to suck his thumb. You think they want a 40-year-old deputy wandering around with his thumb in his mouth?

Five of us in one of those green pickups with a back seat. Four of us crammed together in the rear seat, one in front by the right window. Rhack driving.

And in the middle, that gun.

During the long winding and woodsy ride from camp out to Skyline, Rhack divides his attention, first scanning the landscape with the steely blue eyes of the classic big game hunter, then turning to look down on his gun with tender, beaming affection. In the back seat Sylvester and I enjoy the show.

"Can you dig it?" chuckling deep purple . . . "I can dig it," I tell him.

Nothing pushes a cop's paranoia button quicker than secrets enjoyed at his expense. When we get to the highway Rhack forgets it's deer season and decides to show these wise-ass motherfuckers who's boss of the situation, tromps down on the gas. He's renowned around camp for his drives down the treacherous Highway 84. He likes to get the upper hand by terrifying his passengers screeching around blind curves. Guys arrive in camp round-eyed after their first trip with Rhack—"That bastard is <u>insane</u> behind the wheel!!!"—impressed and cowed by steely blue bravery. But I know 84 too well and have ridden it out too many times with Cassady, and Sylvester just flat has too many scars on his hide to be scared of a couple more. So all the way down we keep the pressure on.

"Ain't he a fantastic driver?" I marvel innocently to Sylvester after a squealing drift.

"Yeah he one of the <u>boss wheel men of all time</u>."

Rhack's in a black mood when we get to Redwood, makes us sit about an hour in the pickup outside the work furlough facilities while he signs over Bewly the bookie. Hot and cramped. One of the guys in the back seat wants to get out and move up front. "Wouldn't," Sylvester advises. "Rhack told me the first day he brang me here: 'You even ack like you run I'll shoot ya.'"

The cars on Bayshore, about 50 yards away—zoom! zoom! zoom! Hot & hazy & vicious. And the Redwood City harbor lovely boats sailing off free into the bay. And on down a ways small planes taking off and passing over us in the lazy sky. Zoom zoom zoom —terribly tempting rivers of freedom roaring past thirsty animals.

> "Beg pardon, lass, but is
> this the road to Brigadoon?"

Finally Rhack comes out and drives the half mile on to the jail. Too late to get to see the doctor today so we're all pissed and complaining. Which creates enough distraction we get in without being searched. I've got pens and notebooks stashed (all the camp jackets have neat little slash pockets in the linings) and Sylvester has zu-zu's and cigarettes and Van Cleve has a hank book.

Back down that corridor, past kitchen, print shop, drunk tank, stand in front of A Tank. "Step back, boys," says the huge fat deputy they call Baby Huey, Ka-SLASH!
                    "Step in, boys—"
KA-SLASH! The speaker in the ceiling is playing "Moon River" 101 Strings.
    Ahhh—Good ole A Tank.

First off, Deputy Gerder sees my pens, busts me for all the colors except the green and my India ink Rapidograph. Gerder is the jail heavy. Flat butch-cut, flat eyes, flat back. He goes heavily past with never a crack. He's good. He takes the whole trip. He knows about watermelon.

"Don't sit there," they tell me—"That door's about to open in a couple minutes."

A Tank
        very low-rent coming going
                    overflowing
                    cons old
                    cons learning
                    Bloods keeping quiet
        and knowing.

"How come we leave camp? How <u>come</u> we leave camp, it being the best of all possible jails?"

"That sounds like Mr. K." It's Breems. "What you doing staying in tank A, Mr. K?"

First off, Deputy Derner sees my pens, busts me for all of the colors except green + my rapidiograph. Derner is the Jail Heavy. Flat brutal flat eyes, flat back he goes heavy past with never a crack. He's good. He takes the whole trip. He knows about watermellon.

"Don't act there," They tell me—

"That show's about to open in a couple minutes."

Too late to see the doctor.

A Tank

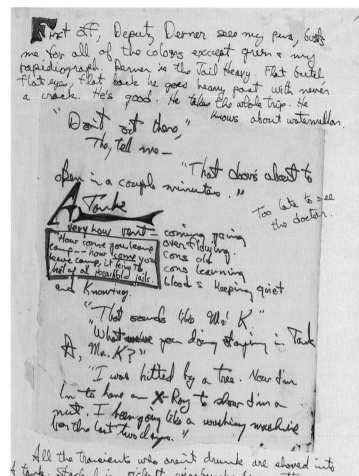

very low rent—coming going over flowing cons old cons learning blood & keeping quiet

"How come you leave camp—how come you leave camp, it bring to best of all possible jails." and knowing.

"That sounds like Mr. K."

"What we're you doing staying in Tank A, Mr. K?"

"I was hitted by a tree. Now I'm I'm to have an X-Ray to show I'm a nut. I been going like a washing machine for the last two days."

All the transient who aren't drunk are shoved into A tank. Stacked in rickety wire bunks bare mattress no sheets no commissary, no shower not even any mother-fucking sugar for this crap they call coffee!

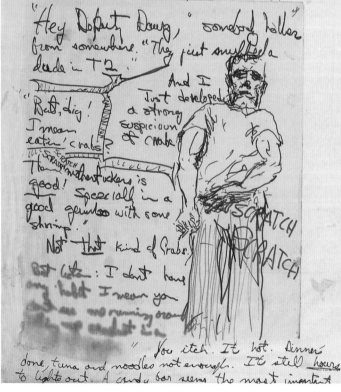

"Hey Deputy Doug," somebody holler from somewhere. "They just snuffed a dude in T 2."

And I Just developed a strong suspicion of crabs

"But, dig! I mean eatin' crabs? Them motherfuckers is good! Special in a good gumbo with some shrimp."

Not that kind of crabs.

But listen: I don't have any habit I mean you are no running around

SCRATCH SCRATCH

"You itch. It hot. Dinner done, tuna and noodles not enough. It's still _hours_ to lights out. A candy bar seems the most important

item in the world.

THE HIPPY in the TANK NEXT DOOR.

"I just moved in, playing my stereo at moderate volume and this motherfucker comes banging on the door. "You gonna play that motherfuckin radio that loud every night."

"Mercy, no, most nights I'm gonna really turn it up."

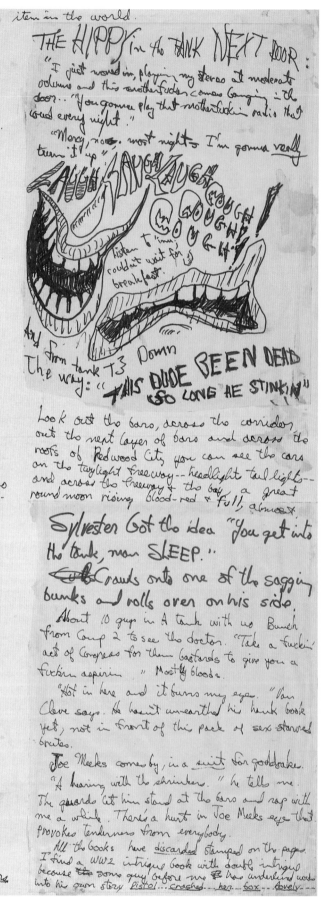

listen t'em; couldn't wait for breakfast.

And from tank T3 down The way: "THIS DUDE BEEN DEAD SO LONG HE STINKIN"

Look out the bars, across the corridor out the next layer of bars and across the roofs of Redwood City you can see the cars on the taylight freeway—headlight tail lights—and across the freeway + the bay, a great round moon rising blood-red & full, almost

Sylvester got the idea "You get into the tank, man SLEEP."

Crawls onto one of the sagging bunks and rolls over on his side.

About 10 guys in A tank with us Bunch from Camp 2 to see the doctor. "Take a fuckin act of Congress for them bastards to give you a fuckin aspirin." Mostly bloods.

"Hot in here and it burns my eyes." Van Cleve says. He hasn't unearthed his hawk book yet, not in front of this pack of sex starved brutes.

Joe Meeks comes by, in a suit for goddsake.

"A hearing with the shrinkers." He tells me. The guards let him stand at the bars and rap with me a while. There's a hurt in Joe Meeks eyes that provokes tenderness from everybody.

All the books have _discarded_ stamped on the pages. I find a WW2 intrigue book with double intrigue because the some guy before me has underlined words into his own story. _pistol... crashed... her... box... lovely_—

"I was hitted by a tree. Now I'm in here to have an x-ray, to see if I cracked my nut or am just nuts. I've been going like a washing machine for the last two days. What you doing in A Tank?"

"Arts and crafts." He holds up a wad of candy wrappers tangled together with dental floss. "This artistic device called a <u>mo</u>-bile."

All the transients who aren't drunk are shoved into **A** Tank. Stacked in rickety wire bunks bare mattresses no sheets no commissary no shower, not even any motherfucking <u>sugar</u> for this crap they call coffee!

"Hey Deputy Dawg," somebody hollers from somewhere. "They just snuffed a dude in T2."

"Hey I just discovered a strong suspicion of crabs. But, dig! I mean <u>eatin' crabs</u>?" Scratch, SCRATCH. "Them motherfuckers is <u>good</u>! Specially in a good gumbo with some shrimp."

"Not <u>that</u> kind of crabs but listen: I don't have any habit I mean you don't see me runnin around scraping toejam and shit try to roll it and smoke it—" Scratch scratch scratch.

You itch you scratch. It's hot. Dinner's done, tuna and noodles not enough. It's still hours and hours until lights out. A candy bar seems the most important item in the world.

The hippie in the tank next door: "I just moved in, playing my stereo at moderate volume and this motherfucker comes banging on the door—'You gonna play that motherfucking stereo that loud every night?' 'Mercy, no. Most nights I'm gonna really turn it up!'"

Laugh laugh ARGH laugh laugh cough cough cough!!! Listen to 'em; can't wait for breakfast. And from tank T3 down the way: "This dude been dead so long he stinkin'."

Look out the bars, across the corridor across the next layer of bars and across the roofs of Redwood City you can see the cars on the twilight freeway—headlights taillights—and across the freeway and the bay, the great round moon rising blood-red and full, almost.

Sylvester got the idea: "You get into the tank, man SLEEP." Crawls onto one of the sagging bunks and rolls over on his side.

About 10 guys in A Tank with us. Bunch from camp to see the doctor. "Take a fuckin' act of Congress for them bastards to give you a fuckin' aspirin." Mostly Bloods.

"Hot in here it burns my eyes." Van Cleve hasn't unearthed his hank book yet, not in front of this pack of sex-starved brutes.

Joe Meeks comes by, in a <u>suit</u> for godsakes! "A hearing with the shrinkers," he tells me. The guards let him stand at the bars and rap with me a while. There's a hurt in Joe Meeks' eyes that provokes tenderness from everybody.

All the books have DISCARDED stamped on the pages. I find a WWII intrigue book with double intrigue because some guy before me has underlined words into his own story: <u>pistol</u> . . . <u>crashed</u> . . . <u>her</u> . . . <u>box</u> . . . <u>lovely</u>.

Don't make the doctor next day either. He's sick. I bitch a little: "I would like to see him before the weekend so I won't miss my visit."

Deputy says "Okay, I'll check on it." Disappears. I wonder just how many have muttered those same magic words then disappeared?

Sylvester is a little less optimistic today. "I wait a certain extent—money eventually goddam me is <u>bound</u> to come my way, someday— <u>some</u> motherfuckin' day . . . **bound to.**"

And a voice comes over the box asks about our welfare then Gerder show up tells us to take down the mobile that Breems made.

"Lighten up, Deputy."

Gurley takes it down and carries it to Gerder. Then back to the "Are you gonna give up your manhood for a million?" debate.

Starved generations rapping hungry at each other's soft spots. "You gonna be a pimp you gonna have to sell you own ass someday."

Finally see the doctor who chats happy with me for-fucking-ever, shows off his fantastic selections of pills in his combination cabinet, tells me I'd best hang around and get an x-ray next week. Time I get back to the tank a hot red moon is peering through the bars.

Smuthers and Johnson and couple other Bloods from camp show up. The moon gets redder and hotter. The Bloods are singing sides from Temptations and Miracles. It's very fucking weird!

Tired dead sniff time. With all the fucking deputies suspecting me of being loaded because I'm taking Valium, some kind of middle mind tranquilizer, and my clothes are dirty and I'm hot and pissed and the paper is even splotchy and I can't sleep because I've got **TIME IS 4:55 TURN IN, TROLLS** and I damn near climb the wall with guilt—oh mosquito, fuck off with you.

Friday night the weekender tenants begin arriving. The star attraction is a plump and outfront fag in tight blue light blue pants. Begins his weekend incarceration by correcting a huge guy playing pinochle, smiling, crossing his legs—"Well, according to the <u>Rules of Hoyle</u> . . ."

All the faces turn toward him. The huge guy grins at his Brothers says "We'll fuck with this dude's mind . . . "

"Not with my mind you won't . . . I dropped two caps of acid before booking in tonight."

The thin mattress pads smell like a lecture in evolution. Gets dreary and dejected and, after a while, a bit crazy. Snores and **hums** of weird electric circuits cough and WHACK lights out late in **A** Tank plus noise and **CLASHINGLING**

tap tap

Tap Tap type scratch **SNORE** HUM SQUeek type type. And the distant whistle of a

Don't make the doctor next day either. He's sick. I bitch a little: "I would like to see him before the weekend so I won't miss my visit."

Deputy says "Okay. I'll check on it." Disappears. I wonder just how many have muttered these magic words and disappeared?

And a voice comes over the box asks about our welfare then Deputy shows up tells us to take the mobile down / that raccoons made "Lighten up, deputy."

Gurley takes it down and carries to Durner. Then back to the "Are you gonna give up your manhood for a million."

Starved generations rapping hungry at each others soft spots. "You gonna be a pimp, you gonna have to sell you own ass someday."

Friday the doctor chats happy with me for a half hour, show off his fantastic selection of pills in his combination cabinet. Tell me I'd best hang around and get an X-Ray next week.

Friday night the weekend tenants arriving. The star, a plump and out-of-front in tight blue light blue pants. Begins by correcting a huge guy playing pinocle. Smiling.

Tired dead sniff time. with all the fucking deputies suspecting me of being loaded because I'm taking valium, some kind of middle mind tranquilizer, and my clothes are dirty and if I'm hot and pissed and the paper is even splotchy and I can't sleep because I've got TIME IS 4·55 TURN IN ROLLS

And I damn near climb the wall with guilt -- oh mosquito, fuck off will you.

crossing his legs -- "Well, according to the rules of Hoyle..." All faces turn toward him. The huge guy says "We'll fuck with this dudes mind..." "Not with my mind you won't... I dropped two caps of acid before booking in tonight."

The thin pads smell like a lecture in evolution.

Gets dreary and dejected and, after a while, a bit crazy

Smothers + Johnson and couple other bloods show up. The moon gets redder and fuller. The bloods are singing from side; Temptations and Miracles. It's very fucking wired!

(I know what they're up to. It's a beautiful scheme. What I get for going for that honesty shit. Send me to the hospital for my head, sure. What he meant was 'stick him down in Redwood until he gets his mind right.)

By the middle of next week I'm resigned to the worst, things are so heavy I'm goofy.

"I don't like to be booked, but I don't like to be taken up with neither so what the hell."

There's things you learn in jail boy like what the truth is and why you keep shut about it!

And Chandler has smuggled in some colored pens and candy bars. And Jerry Govier is loaded with gossip.

deputy coming closer JINGLING his **KEYS** type type——type——type "**NO GUTS NO GUTS!**" Says one of the unknown

Bloods somewhere in one

of the other unknown

TANKS

Toss and turn over hack and *swching* of keys in locks going away.

(I know what they're up to. It's a beautiful scheme. What I get for that honesty shit. Send me to the hospital for my head, sure. What they meant was "Stick him down in Redwood until he gets his <u>mind</u> right.")

TRY SEE try **YELL!** Snap your fingers Come on and Move Sing fallout callout BALLout "I don't

like to be broke but I

don't like to be locked up neither

so what the hell . . . "

"There's things you learn in jail, boy, like what the truth is and why you keep still about it!"

BUT even as I pick up the **GOOD BOOK** and cut into old John a CHANGE is on its way to good old tank A. Chandler has smuggled in some colored pens and candy bars.

Gerder comes by and busts Chandler for his whole set of pens.

"Ain't that a bitch . . . but at least he missed my outfit."

Gossip from the camp: 70 half-gallons of milk came into the kitchen on Wednesday, only five were left on Thursday. Who's the culprit of this dire deed? Captain Queeg wants to know. Sergeant Wayne wants to know. And finds an empty milk bottle on the back porch of C Barracks, <u>also</u> an empty cornflakes box. "We was framed," says C Barracks. "We'll see about that," says Wayne. "We're taking prints on that bottle and checking with Redwood. And the men with it hanging over them better get ready to ride a burglary beef."

(Two deputies walking past: "Yeah, I broke it." "Scope and all?" "Scope, stock, barrel and all—and right after I saw a forked horn in the three point area." "Some days are just pure bad luck.")

Anyway the milk is finally hung on Fruit, the paranoid tomcat that lives under our barracks.

Then who else is in Redwood this very night but Hoihoi Henry, the very man Breems split camp to avoid. Seems that Henry took offenses to having Breems sit in the car with his wife's sister during visiting day while Henry's wife visited. I'd watched some of it.

Breems don't smoke but he likes zu-zu's, anything sweet—Snickers, lollipops, sugar cubes—and he don't sing the familiar sides with the other Bloods like the Miracles and the

Temptations—just watches quiet and cool out from under his thin blue specs—a thin black flower child with no place to plant his roots.

So when Samurai Henry, the bad dude of the whole camp, says "You stay out of my wife's car," and slim little Breems don't quake a quiver but says instead "Man, you don't know who you're talking to like that"—it kind of makes the fellas wonder just who exactly is this weird blue dude that Henry is talking to like that?

But Henry presses on. And Breems keeps coming back smart-ass weird cool saying "You don't know what I got for you," in his Mau Mau purr, and the fellas saying "Hit him, Henry, bust him, Henry" until Henry hits him and they go to tussling and somehow Henry gets his finger hung in Breems' shirt and Breems spins away and tells Henry "I hope you busted the motherfucking thing!"

And Henry, looking in amazement at his pinkie which is jammed all the way back into his big samurai hand, says "It looks like I did bust the motherfucking thing."

That was when Breems put in a request to come to Redwood to confer with the Public Defender. Now Henry has finally come in to see the doctor about his finger. Along with his sweetie, Chandler, who's come down to have his blood dry-cleaned as a result of a dirty needle.

MORNING—   The Limelighters tell us about
                    "This land is your land
                    This land is my land glory hallelujah—"

and this old dude's telling about how his wife used to be a good thief a good thief until she started shooting crystal.

I been fucking near a week in here waiting for x-rays and if I don't get finished and outta here with Rhack this afternoon I'm gonna . . . uh . . . gonna . . . yeah, right.

Dear Faye:

This land was made for you and me reaches an apocalyptic climax on station KPEN . . . And the morning sun comes rattling through the bars like a high caliber repeater while we wait for our morning mush . . . still in A Tank, still waiting unshaven and forlorn to have my head x-rayed (a tree hit me on the head, um let's see, it must have been two weeks now "zip-a-dee-do-da")—I saw the doctor and he scheduled an x-ray— so here it fucking is Friday and if I don't get it this morning I miss visiting day and I languish, suffering the weekend away in old tank A—but our mush has arrived at least.

Receiving: baddest vibes stored up after millennia of waiting, to get in, to get out, to get through.

Down the spine the ratchet sound of a pair of prisoners cuffed together: "But what about my call?"

"Hang on."

"Man, I just get me my call and call my wife she's <u>waiting</u> with the bond."

"Hang on."

"I been in since—"

"Hang on! If you don't like the service then don't come in here!"

The final word. Wait.

WAIT!

Deputy Johnson gets us (finally) back from (finally) x-ray . . . Two o'clock Friday afternoon. Has Rhack left for camp yet? Do I have to spend <u>another</u> weekend locked from the light of day? It's beginning to look like it. I start work on an SOS . . . then Rhack shows and I make it back for the big meeting after all and meet the Pranksters for refueling—glory glory.

Love, Ken

RUMBLE RUMBLE RUMBLE

Allen says, sniveling about A Tank, "When they take you into that jail, you're treated like a common criminal."

Sheriff Honor Camp
Somewhere in Woods
Summertime
Sixty Seven

Sir Speed Limit
c/o Brian Rohan
Attorney Out Law
1818 Octavia, SF

Neal:

Here's a little Paul Robertson snapshot you and Rohan ought to appreciate. After numerous legal briefs that don't happen plus red herrings that do, Robertson shows up in this Lotus convert that George has painted up all sykadelic dayglo paisley purtified. He's got a dark necktie unloosened and cool, and a bright topdown burn on his ivory dome. He's also got this knockout young lovely nestled on the leather bucket seat beside him. And I mean knock you down and <u>out</u>!

She's oozing out of a skintight Hawaiian frock like some kinda irrepressible tropical fruit, early ripening. Her peachy skin is lit from behind by a glow both innocent and lascivious. Her blond hair is cut close and casual. Her eyes are empty pools awaiting unknown possibilities. Her mouth is puckered and drooling at the thought of all the dangerous delights this campful of horny men must have to offer.

She waits in the convertible while Paul and I go over papers he has spread out on the car's swirly hood—all spread out herself. She puts on a pair of rainbow shades to protect herself but all involved can see she simply <u>loves</u> the impact she is having on these poor deprived souls. She stretches and lolls. Finally the leather is Oh <u>too</u> sweaty, what with several hundred eyeballs lapping at her from the rows of men in line for supper— so she climbs out, over the door, one milk-fed leg after the other. And she's <u>barefoot</u>! A mutual groan of raw suffering lust rises from mutually slavvering mouths "Oooo," because now everybody in camp can see that—except for one teensy gold ring on one teensy toe— this nubile beauty is <u>barefoot</u> all the way up under that tropical print and on out the top clear to the sunglasses!

I swear, Neal, if this naked-tootsied tootsie had been redheaded instead of blond, even cool-and-collected you would not have been able to hold yourself back.

She tippytoes tenderly to the rear of the Lotus and resumes her lolling with a will. She blows down her bosom. She arches backward to allow the sun a better peek. She pulls the dresstop out a couple inches to let the little breezes feel around. And just when you think you can't stand it any longer our old German shepherd, Con, lifts his grizzled muzzle and howls, inconsolable. The men take up the howl. Finally Sergeant Wayne comes tromping through the ice plants to tell Paul that his consultation time is over.

"We've got to get these men fed, Mr. Robertson."

Paul says "We were just finished, Constable." He piles papers back into his briefcase, then extracts a doe-skinned book. "Except for this Bible I've brought up to guide our wayward boy back to the straight and narrow. Could you give it to him after you check it over good of course?"

The book's cover is dove white in Wayne's rasty old paws. He riffles once through it and hands it to me with one of his Marine Corps grunts. Paul ladles his melting lollipop back into the Lotus. After he whirrs the Lotus to life he puts on his shades and calls out for me and the whole camp, too, to hear: "I marked you a passage you'll be interested in . . . in the book of Revelations at the end. Chapter 13, verse 18. Look it up."

The Lotus takes a slow victory lap around the ice plants and eases away toward the gate. A lingering scent of forbidden fruit trailing behind. Suddenly the smell is overthrown by a blast of Brut aftershave, and there's this smarmy sonofabitch named Szikso sidled up alongside me.

"Mmm-mmm!" He holds like invisible in his two hands a big peach. "Wouldn't you like to pry that open and smooch!—right where it's brown?"

He pantomimes the act in movement so nasty it makes the whole wicked dumbshow feel filthy. The bell rings chow but I've somehow lost my appetite. What an unwholesome little devil! Szikso is one of the camp's ironpile devotees, a head shorter than the other weightlifters. He's often in the shower room, reeking of Brut and flexing with the big fellows. "It ain't the mass that chicks dig; it's the delineation."

Flex flex.

The biggest thing on him is his jaw. It's a giant's jaw, stitched onto a dwarf by some sick Frankenstein surgeon. The black guys call him Sosick instead of Szikso. But it's worse than that . . .

When I get around to the Bible Paul left and check the Revelation verse, it's the one about the Number of the Beast. And Szikso's bunk number is sixty-six.

Boogity boogity. We got to watch out for nasty curves on this tricky road we weave.

Love, Ken

From the lower area where Page scrubs his clothes at the edge of the pool and Chandler and the Blood who wants to know "How 'bout making a million dollars collaborating with me, man?" . . . from the swale of bay and redwood and that one lone tropical whatya-magig around the pool, comes the agonized beauty of Prokofiev suffering its way uphill to me, past the redwoods, the bay trees and the grove of heavy machinery off to my right where they are clearing the land. "Soon, all thees, all thees trees, all, be underwater—again," is Speedy's prediction.

The jays compete with Prokofiev. The morning sun rises. The utility crew fucks off furtively, awaiting the arrival of Max, the man who will give us a more definite job than simply fucking off. Yet we must keep an eye peeled for him; perhaps if we can hop to it suddenly enough to look industrious when he shows he won't bother us but leave us to push a lackadaisical broom until Rhack arrives. Who knows what will be wrought upon us by this day's Hand of Justice?

Prokofiev ends the 1st (of his 5th) reeling a bit and takes off tipsily through the trees.

Work Bus

Old Deputy Carl Finestra with heavy suspicion: "They's somebody smokin' in the back this bus. Catch him we rip five days."

Pete, at the wheel, suggests "Take the names of everybody on the left side and make 'em work Saturday."

"Cause they's somethin' smokin' on this here bus."

What they don't know is it's them that's smokin' and what Pete smelled (besides his driving) was an apple core tossed out the window glimpsed in his left-hand mirror, and created an olfactory hallucination of nicotine.

And Pete's driving gets worse.

"Let Carl drive!" somebody hollers.

"Carl can't drive," Chandler explains. "His feet won't reach the pedals."

So Pete goes on, bogarting the poor bus and muttering "Flagrant violation" to Carl; Carl tries to cool him, talks him out of gigging everybody on the left side of the bus.

But there's still more laughter. More jouncing. Pete gets more rattled. Carl more uptight. Because it ain't him they's laughing at, it's the driver, his employer, his <u>county</u>. And if nothing else Carl is loyal. Trying to clean up behind a job of bum driving. He can't understand the laughter. Men begin to pretend to smoke, to act like they're passing joints back and forth. There's jokes being played that he ain't in on and everybody else is. Because we all saw it was the apple core that Pete glimpsed but nobody is letting them in on the joke.

Then—by God—after we're back to the barracks one of the guys from the <u>left</u> side of the bus confides in me that he <u>had</u> been smoking.

So Carl smelled cigarette smoke after all, even if Pete had seen only an apple core.

So we were all wrong.

And the joke was on everybody.

I'm in the dayroom holding forth on entropy and how it is eroding people's belief in God and so on—

"Entropy is the anarchy of sunshine off a chrome bumper. Entropy is Owsley's story of the runaway train, highballing down a steep grade, overloaded with passengers without any knowledge of the tight turn coming up at the bottom of the hill. But we're on top of the train in the Indian cheap seats, and we can see the curve a-comin' and can feel by the seat of our pants that we are not! going to! make it! So we split into two action groups—one group to go down inside the train and apprise the passengers of the doom impending and try to stir them into doing something about it; the other to work their way to the front of the train and, if they don't feel the train slowing down, blow the tracks before the curve, and let the train go steaming into the trackless."

"Oh, I see," Fassenaux comes in-chiming with impeccable timing. "It's like how a man's family always gets to be more than he can cope with, until he must needs throw his head back and holler at the sky: 'Lordgawdamighty, give us a <u>hand</u> here!' I see. It ain't a belief in God that we lack. We have plenty of faith that God exists . . . we just ain't sure He's going to be able to cope."

Religion begins to rear its head . . .

CHRIST
pulled time
for ALL you motherfuckers
SO LIGHTEN UP ON
EACH OTHER

Deputy Write stops me coming outta the mess hall; "Kesey . . . I want you to drop into my office tonight. It's time we talked."

Write (or is it "Wright?") 30-something, ex-marine and overweight. The kind of hard overweight that takes hikes after supper to keep in trim. Known as a camp "heavy" for his strict adherence to the rules.

"Wright would as leave gig you as look at you," I'm informed. "And them little talks in his office? They a real bitch."

So I sweat and fret one hour, two hours, three hours until I'm finally called over the speaker. (In this way, you understand, you can be made to pull "double-time" or even "triple-time," sweating what you've done and what's gonna be done with you as well as what you're doing.) Wright is seated behind the desk nervously clearing his throat. We hem and haw about family and such before he finally gets into it and asks with pious tone:

"Kesey . . . about this LSD; does it ever give you any—uh—religious experiences?"

Religion Begins to Rear its head

CHRIST DIED THAT FOR ALL (you MotherFuckers) SO LIGHTEN UP ON EACH OTHER

RELIGIOUS EXPERIENCE

What can you do for a cop who wants a FLASH?

I believed WRIGHT. He is the typical Christian servant who, after years of faithful brute service, would like a little taste of the CREAM. But his rule book doesn't permit him to take chemical shortcuts. He is sincere, of good heart and is asking to be turned on, yet dope is out of the question. All you can do is try to reassure that "hang on, Sloopy; the Man you are working for has a pretty good reputation for rewarding services rendered."

DEPUTY WRITE

Stops me coming outta the mess hall:

"Kesey...I want you to drop in to my office tonight. It's time we talk."

Write (or is it "Wright"?) is 30-something, ex-marine and overweight. A kind of hard, red-rubber overweight that takes hikes after supper to keep in trim. Known as the camp "Heavy" for his strict adherence to the rules.

"Wright would as leave gig you as look at you," I'm informed. "And the little talks in his office? A real bitch."

So I sweat and fret one hour, two hours three hours until I'm finally called over the speaker (in this way, you understand, you can be made to pull "double-time," or even "triple-time", sweating what you've done and what's gonna be done with you as well as what you're doing) Wright is seated behind a desk, nervously clearing his throat. We him and haw about family + such before he finally gets down to it:

"Kesey... about this LSD: did it ever give you any—uh—Religious Experience?"

YOU CAN'T LOVE 'EM ALL

UNLESS

RELIGIOUS
EXPERIENCES?

WHAT can you do for a cop who wants a >**FLASH**< ?

I believe Wright's pious tone. He's the typical Christian servant who, after years of faithful brute service, would like a little taste of the CREAM. But his rule book doesn't permit him to take chemical shortcuts. He's sincere of good heart and is unwittingly asking to be turned on, yet dope is out of the question. All you can do is try to reassure the good and faithful servant. "Hang on, Sloopy; the Man you are working for has a pretty good reputation for rewarding services rendered."

SATURDAY NIGHT

After lights out transistor radios up near black ears. Turned low but loud enough you can hear them all together: "Can you XERB, dig it, brother?" Wolfman Jack's dirty voice smuggled across the border clear into this twisted hideaway . . . "Gonna rip it up! (bimp, bump), gonna shake it up . . ." "Have mercy; Lil' Richard—" "Havin' a ball tonight."

"Eeeyooo dat's Lil' Ricardo," Wolfman howls; "Now I'm wearin' a Wolfman Jack spankin' new T shirt. Dis yere T shirt got a actual photo of the Wolfman . . . a actual photo wear to yo' softball games an' such . . . send two dollars along wif your size to station **XERB Holl-EE-wood Cal-EE-forn-EE-<u>AAA</u>!**"

Rock moved up the river, gathering the moss of America as it rolled because it was no ordinary rolling stone: enough truth and ego bein' beat into it to create its own gravitational field drawing bitter blood out of Kansas City, the heart, picking up the mechanical piston in Detroit . . . coming across the bleak dusty flat country to the sea again to add the everlasting wash and roll of the ocean wave.

I don't like to sing into a twisted ear. The cup beneath the water shapes the turning of the tap. Let me scrub a little place my feet to flip and flap.

And dance a beat free of muddy fear.

ROCK! Rock. Comes from Rock to Blues. To Jazz. To R&B and finally from Swing this Hammer back to that same old Rock.

Of ages.

Can you dig it.

San Mateo Sheriff Camp
Skyline Blvd #666
Skylonda, Calif

Dead Digs
710 Ashbury
San Fran, Calif

Hey Jerry:

I get another permission to use the electric in the camp office.

So this is another episode in the ongoing saga of Breems, the Black Flowerchild Acid Head With the Thin Blue Shades. As you will recall we left our young hero in hot water again, after being swung on by Samurai Henry when Henry scopes him making moves on his sister-in-law in the parking lot. Turns out Henry's finger wasn't broke after all—just dislocated. And this gets Henry off Bushie's road crew and replaced with Breems.

So things work out.

Anyway we get back from a dusty gritty sweaty day of chipper work. We're late. Bushie's truck wouldn't start. Dead battery. Breems had turned the truck's radio on, figuring Bushie would never know because he wears earplugs when working around the snarling shrieking howling chipper (we're all supposed to wear them) and he was right. Bushie never noticed all day long . . . until he went to start the truck.

So Bushie tries to call the camp for help. But of course, with the truck's battery dead the shortwave doesn't work either. I direct him to a house I know of across the road (reason I know is because I bummed a couple aspirin there, but that's another story).

By the time we get back to camp and check in our tools it's after six. We head for the barracks to get a shower and find that our lazy lard-ass housemother Welah has been cleared for work furlough. Deputy Rhack had already driven him down to Redwood City and now informs us, grinning and simpering as though he had a mouth full of canaries, that our new housemother is Sylvester—who's standing there in front of the latrine door, shirtless, arms crossed, feet spread, like some Nubian guard. To call him black doesn't even come close. Eggplant purple is more like it. Fireplug short and just as solid, with a nasty scar slanting all the way from his brow to his throat.

Sylvester and I have spent some time together in trucks and the tank, but we haven't talked and I don't know his story. Later the dorm is empty except for Golden and me, getting our shaving kits and towels. I don't say anything but Goldie can see I'm itching with curiosity. "Sylvester used to be a easy-going dude, they say," Goldie tells me. "Nice family, job, house. Then he lose it all in a arson fire. Some claim it was cops didn't like him on the white side of the freeway, some even say it was some brothers, didn't like it him living there, either. Only thing anybody know for sure is since then he don't take no shit—not from the bulls not from the brothers nor nobody. Thing is the more shit he don't take the more comes his way."

"How did he get that scar?"

Goldie gives me a look. "Well now, just how do you s'pose he got that scar, Home? He got cut, is how"—and heads for the dayroom.

Breems and Smuthers are already there, pleading their case. Rhack's gone and Sylvester is standing just like we left him.

"We got to get this poison oak rinsed off," Smuthers explains.

"Yeah, man," Breems chimes in.

"Won't take but a second."

"Yeah, man," insists Breems. "I'm known as the Thin Blue Flash! And I be fast, know what I'm saying? <u>Whoosh</u>, I'm in there! <u>Zing</u>, I'm shaved! <u>Whiz</u>, I'm out! what I'm trying to tell you man is I be one fleetfooted nonstop <u>fast</u> motherfucker!"

"The Man run the rules down to me motherkillin clear—" (and I swear Sylvester's voice is as deep purple as his skin) "and the rules say no showers between 6 PM and 8 PM. And, Mister Breems—no matter how fast you be . . . I can be just . . . that . . . slow."

Golden doesn't say anything until we've trudged our way to the mess hall door. "That gloomy motherfucker got slow confused with heavy. I bet his shadow weigh ninety pounds."

Ooop! Speaking about "The Man" here comes Sergeant J. Wayne! More later . . .

Maybe,

Keez

What if, let's say, you're a two-hundred-year-old Blood who never aged physically past 20? (<u>I seen me a lot of bad shit</u>.) And what if, in the accumulation of your experience, you conclude that the <u>wisest</u> survival under circumstances is an attitude of forced detachment? (<u>I seen the lotus and I seen the shit which it growed outta</u>). The result of your conclusion produces first a cool front, a looseness, a hipness, even a little <u>natural rhythm</u> until <u>finally</u> you achieve your machined detachment (<u>man, I'm fuckin *spaced*</u>). You've learned what it takes years of police work to teach you—you've learned the most important jailhouse lesson and most valuable underground skill—you've learned how to

HOLD

YOUR

MUD

(<u>I mean any dumb motherfucker goes around getting his button pushed and his covers pulled is a motherfucking duck!</u>)

(<u>you know?</u>)

SO you hold it. Play it cool and passive. And you wait. You see injustice but you don't snivel. Pretty soon you don't even sing the blues. You can't jive with the younger Bloods anymore because that would mean letting go, and there's so much mud dammed back now it would all come boiling out if you slacked off. And your upper lip gets stiff. Convict lip, they call it. And your eyelids droop into slits. And you learn how to walk

WHAT IF, Let's say, you're a two-hundred year-old Blood who never aged physically past twenty? (I seen me a lotta bad shit) And what if, in the accumulation of your experience, you conclude that the wisest survival under circumstance is an attitude of forced detatchment? (I seen the lotus and I seen the shit what it grow'd outta.) The result of your conclusion produces first a cool front, a looseness, a hip ness, even a little Natural Rythm until finally you achieve your machined detatchment (man, I'm fuckin spaced). You've learned what it takes years of police work to teach you, the most important jail house lesson and most valuable underground skill:

how to **HOLD YOUR MUD!**

(I mean, any dumb motherfucker goes around gettin his button pushed and his covers pulled is a motherfuckin DUCK!)

(You know?)

So, you hold it. Play it cool and passive. And you wait. You see injustice but you don't snivvle. Pretty soon you don't even sing the blues. You can't jive with the younger bloods any more because that would mean letting go, and there so much mud dammed back now it would all come boiling out if you slacked off. And your upper lip gets stiff. Convict's lip. And your eyelids droop into slits. And you learn how to walk slow and drink a lot of water. And it gets hard to get your nut. And you hold it. And wait.

SYLVESTER W. S. OUR HOUSE mother. The man of C Barrack's old Welch. ("Tired of us eatin' heart, that mother fucker plays hearts!") Sylvester dumped the job due to his bad eye keeping him off the road work. When he was assigned as his fat-assed (Barracks, he chuckled ironically) off the "Better'n diggin garbage pits," and decided with a detatched efficiency, that first put us back to work it first place in the lunch line. Nat that he actually worked much harder than Welch, but once he got the place clean nobody came in to mess around until the deputies had inspected. Welch, nervous, sensitive, chubby and a little paranoid, couldn't command this kind of respect. Nobody, not even old Cambell, wanted to go against Sylvester's person.

And I'm laying there in my rack. With a head ache and a lay-in ("Mr. Crossfield, my head still aches where that tree got me.") and mainly an acid hangover. Watching Sylvester move along between the rows of bunks, tidying and prempting for inspection; humming along with Sweets radio.
"What the beef you're doing," I ask him
He give me a look. Hardly a half-second Then runs his charge down to me. Strong arm. Assault. One of those things that Bloods do. I forget.
But I remember the look Asking me. "Are you kidding?"

"I mean you jivin' me, man?"

89

slow and drink a lot of water. And it gets hard to catch your nut. And you hold it. And wait.

SYLVESTER is now our housemother. All us men of C Barracks had wanted to dump old Welah: ("Tired of us eatin' last while the fat-assed motherfucker plays hearts!") but Welah got furloughed out. Sylvester was given the job due to his bad eye keeping him off the roadwork crew. When he was assigned janitor of C Barracks he chuckled ironically and decided "Better'n diggin' garbage pits," and set to work with a detached efficiency that put us back in first place in the lunch line. Not that he actually worked much harder than Welah. But once he got the place clean, nobody came in to mess around until the deputies had inspected. Welah, nervous, sensitive, chubby and a little paranoid, couldn't command this kind of respect. Nobody, not even old Fassenaux, wanted to go against Sylvester's grain.

I'm lying there in my rack. With a headache and a lay-in. And mainly an acid hangover. Watching Sylvester move along between the rows of bunks, tidying and primping for inspectors, humming along with Sweet's radio.

"What's the beef you're doing?" I ask him in token attempt to act neighborly.

He gives me a look. Hardly a half second. One eye burning the other yolk yellow and leaking down that knife scar . . . A look, half scolding that I come on so whitebread, half sad that this is the way it has to be. Then runs his charge down to me in that slow purple voice. Strong-arm assault. One of those things that Bloods do. I forget. But I remember the look asking me without words:

"Are you <u>kidding</u>? I mean you <u>jivin'</u> me, man?"

BITCH!

She ain't a woman ain't even a human actually.

She just a white lie pasted inside you locker . . . She a hank book under you pillow . . . She on TV and she sometime in you bed. But not usually the way you wish she was. Ooooo! . . . kiss it for me, little one . . .

. . . ooo, hurry, hurry!

We're a bunch of us sitting around the TV watching a young lovely finish up her song on the Jack Paar show . . . and she's offering everything in a breakaway white gown inspiring Breems to declare "That my bitch." He puts both hands in the air. "All the rest of you tramps keep back because she stood right there and promised me some shit."

                                                                    Be with

                                                                    you in a

                                                                    sec, kid.

Szikso says "Breems you be sweet but you ain't <u>ever</u> get that far uptown."

Breems says "Uptown or back alley I know a promise."

Sylvester soft and purple laugh—"Yeah an' you try to collect on that promise someday black boy, an' you won't get off easy as Trail did."

Trail flares at the back dig and fires back. "Easy? A year isn't what I call easy."

"No," Sylvester says, "but sweet Breems here would pull ten."

Trail lets it drop. We watch the TV singer.

"A promise is a promise," Breems says.

                                                    HANK BOOK

is the

                                                    term for

PLAYBOY

                                        & NUGGET & ADAM and

                                        new

                                        comers like

                                        BLACKLEATHER and

BLOODSTUD and

                                                    GNAW!

Just hank books. No big thang. Cops and cons alike collect them, read them, hide them . . . all the pussy you gonna <u>git</u> til you <u>hit</u> the street, Sweet!

"A promise is a promise," Breems says again.

Tick tick **tick TOCK . . .**

Just in case we'd better de-activate. Check the vermature control, turn down the famamold, damn and see the magna-pole doesn't oscillate ZAM packa packa PACKA

SNAP!

Stand BACK Look OUT oh **NO!** —- Too late. After the sufficient period circled the particular **Time . . .** don't y**OU** re**CALL?**

the thUNDERSTORM?!?

Ah-haw! . . . Well, it finally struck!

I'm about half straightened up when I hear the party trembling our direction. **BUBBLE** It's Henry after Chandler.

"You don't need no diploma from no college," Chandler giggles, "to see how acid will pop a pig bladder."

Then Feretti and Sweet, then Trail, rip-roaring after them through our barracks tossing a ball.

BUBBLE! Then five minutes and all of them back through, Henry carrying under one arm Chandler red-cheeked and jelly-bellied wearing nothing but a monocle and a black glove . . . And Feretti dashing behind to spray them all with a fire extinguisher. Bostic and Sweet and Trail following **TOIL AND** slippering everywhichaway on the wet floor laughing too wild too messy good thing Sylvester's over in the office getting his medications and eye-drops **MEANWHILE** we're all trying to get them to cool down. But how can you cool down when Daly City Louie Chandler is giggling pink jelly drunk in C Barracks' dayroom? Everybody following to see except Kirby playing solitaire, and me, and, finally (why the hell not?) me.

On red-plastic couch Henry and Trail raslin' Chandler, me trying to draw him with paintpens slobbering all over this notebook's fire-extinguisher-drenched pages.

Chandler is hilarious, flashing falling giggling everybody's certain the staff will hear the ruckus over the squawk box and come tearing over and ship the whole barracks to Redwood City. But the staff doesn't hear. They're probably gathered around the pinochle table, listening to Szikso mumble cryptic snitch gossip.

Sunday night movie is announced: "The classic horse opera, SHANE"—spurring Chandler on to new drunken heights EeeeHAW! Bunks 72–99 are called to small group. That's me. Damn. On the way to the office I run into Sylvester with clean white eye bandage. "How's things, Home?" he rumbles.

"Things are fine," I lie, hurrying up steps. Seated around the table with 20 guys. Small room. With windows open. Door open. Can see Rhack in the mess hall trying to load the movie into the projector. The talk's about Goldie's modification shot. Should he go for it or no? Give reasons. Everybody keeps talk up loud and enthused, hoping to cover the racket, exchanging glances of concern for pandemonium outside. Uproar increasing. Everybody wondering: "How can these two bulls not hear it?" Spreading through the barracks, A to B to C and back to B . . . gets a bit quieter, may be cooled down . . . no, now a yell—"No laughing, motherfucker!" Can't believe Givens and Rhack don't hear shouts **mad KILL** the fight FIGHT! **waste** the mother**FUCKER** rising in the night.

Then, in the very nick, Rhack has the projector working, announces over the squawk box, "Sunday movie will be starting in five minutes in the mess hall—one of America's greatest western flicks, *Shane*."

"Them westerns ain't so great to this cat," Breems declares. "The redskins never win."

Prompting Rhack to lean again to the mike, "Attendance not I repeat <u>not</u> mandatory."

The hullabaloo continues. It can be heard over the movie's soundtrack blaring from the mess hall's blown speakers. Everybody can hear it except Rhack and Givens. They're sitting right next to the grindy old Bell & Howell projector, absolutely engrossed. They can't even hear the dark roomful of men laughing behind their backs.

They might have missed the riot altogether had the projector bulb not burned out just as Shane and Jack Palance were fixin' to get down to it!

"What's that?" Givens asks.

"I don't know," says Rhack, flipping on the mess hall lights, "but I think it's trouble!"—the night outside surging scrambling around shouting, trash-mouthing. The deputies look at each other, suddenly dumbstruck by a dawning realization: they are the only guards at the camp this Sunday eve. Two guards, and 100 prisoners, divided right down the middle: 50 white and 50 black!—then Chandler busts through the double screen doors wearing nothing but a dingy terrycloth robe and a perplexed expression.

"Are all of you gentlemen unaware of the situation we have on our hands?" "Nope, only them two gentlemen wearing badges," Fassenaux answers. "The rest of us, we are aware sonofaguns." "Shut up Fassenaux," Rhack orders. "What sort of situation, Mr. Chandler?" "The riot sort." "Yeah what kind of riot?" "The race riot kind." "Mau mau," Breems purrs. "Where is it?" "Where is what?" "This race riot?" "Everywhere, can't you hear it?" Feretti comes shouting through the screen doors: "Fight!" "Who?" "Bostic and Sylvester." "What happened?" "Well, Deputy Rhack," Chandler begins, "it seems that Mr. Sylvester objected to the waterfight which—" "Yeah, Sylvester! That one-eyed nigger came up from behind and clubbed Bostic in the face with an AX!" "Did what?" "Clubbed Bostic in the face—" "From behind?" "Who did you say—?" "Sylvester! Sylvester, that motherfucking one-**eyed NIGGER!**"

THOSE NIGGERS ARE USING AXES!

And just like that the room is divided, Blacks on one side, Whites on the other.

RACE RIOT!

Got nothing against the Niggers. My own
wife's a fucking Nigger. But she never hit me
with no AX . . .

Man believe FIGHT FAIR until coupla healthy
experiences wake him up or do him in . . .
then man believe JUST FIGHT because that
what the man believe that taught
him! And I believe a fight is not no
Fun and Games and soons I decide
well looks like it going to be . . . I go
on get DOWN WITH IT even I gots
to KILL some motherfucker!

He right. He is right. Any dude done much
street fighting tell you: No such thing as
FAIR! Not in a street fight. But still and all . . .

Trail and me together couldn't pull him off
Bostic . . . a crazied APE.

Weren't doing a thing and he comes
down with an AX!

Deputy Givens sir, I know Feretti sounds
like he's stretching it some but sir, I
was sitting right there and it's every
word of it the Gospel truth! . . . Bostic
was just sitting there on his bed as we
do in the evenings, drinking coffee with
Feretti when that ONE-EYED NIGGER
for NO REASON anybody could see . . .

Except the motherfucker is SOAKED
from the water he squirted all over
SYLVESTER's area—an' Sylvester,
decent, AST him to clean it an' Bostic says
"Fuck off, Nigger, I'm too drunk to do
decent!"

A little bit of water. LITTLE WATER ain't
any reason to use an ax on a man!

Weren't doing <u>nothing</u>? Sylvester just
finished mopping out you mess in the dayroom before Bostic come TEARING ASS
through with a fire extinguisher again like . . .
some asshole kid with a bunch . . .

Nobody's saying we weren't fucking off
a little . . . but it takes a <u>dirty</u> Nigger

O.K. Trail, let's just lighten up on the mouth
before . . .

to go for an ax over a water
fight. I mean who but a Nigger would
have that kinda head?

I said GET OFF THAT TALK
<u>MOTHERFUCK</u>

RUMBLE   RUMBLE   RUMBLE

E A R T H Q U A K E !

Dear Faye:

We had a race riot last week. Didn't exactly start out that way, though ever since they got the still up on the hill going again some of the inmates been getting looser and looser, the Bloods more and more irritated at their lack of cool. Anyway, Chandler and Bostic and some others were frolicking around our barracks like a giddy drunken bunch of school kids with the teacher out of the room, squirting the fire extinguisher and making a general soggy mess out of our dayroom—just spic-n-span cleaned by Sylvester our house-mother. Not a prudent move.

The rest of us were in the mess hall watching SHANE, aware of the ruckus and the hell to pay when Sylvester returned, when the projector bulb burned out and the hell to pay came rushing in at us—first yelling, then the door busting open and Chandler declaring "RIOT!" and Feretti behind him shouting "Bostic and Sylvester are fighting!" and Trail pushing through them both, "Hit him in the face with an ax!" . . . "Who?" "Sylvester! That motherfucking one-eyed Nigger!"

I didn't see anyone move, yet suddenly whites were on one side of the room, blacks on the other—big loud yelling, tension building, but then a funny thing. There were hawks and doves on both sides, and the hawks could only yell at one another, baiting, raising the ante, ready to strike. But the doves could talk across the divide to the doves on the other side, and between them they started smoothing things out a bit. And just then, while we're at this kind of impasse, the floor started shaking—lights swinging, rumble of a freight train bearing down on us. It was an honest to God earthquake . . . Like God himself reached down and got us all by the collar and said "You want to see riot? . . . I'll show you RIOT!" Or was it the power from beneath, sifting us like wheat?

It brought the riot to an end. Reinforcements were called in and Sylvester was hauled off to S.F. prison, the others involved to County Jail and Bostic to be doctored. Sylvester had hit him with the handle end of the ax, laid him out good. But I hear he's already back in B Tank in Redwood City.

Yesterday, Breems and Golden saw me throwing the I Ching and wanted to give it a try. So I gave them the coins and they threw #51, The Arousing—Shock, Thunder.

 The Arousing, Thunder

The Arousing, Thunder

Shock brings success

Shock comes—oh oh!

Laughing words—ha ha!

The shock terrifies for a hundred miles,

And he does not let fall the sacrificial spoon and chalice.

And that night it did thunder—our first thunderstorm. And we'd already had a riot. Thunder over Thunder—ummm—ohhhh—maybe we just leave this alone . . .

I've enclosed the first episode of a children's story I've been thinking about. This seed that gets blown and/or carried around to these many adventures. Read it to the kids. I'll write them separate letters later. Might be fun writing children's stories.

Luv, Ken

JAILPOME

I grow up
I get famous
I take dope.
I behold mercy.
I learn how to
put my arm
around the shoulders
of a bent over friend
but I never really
know what it means until
a son dies
And still
that's just
the top of it.

We are
embarked on a course
charted by genius,
revolutionary genius
(see Tom Paine)
and that's still
just the top of it.

We hear
the gray gay ringing
of tears as Walt
Whitman walks the bloody
mud of our ripped and
colored flesh . . .
and that's still
just the grizzly
glimmering
ghastly top of it.

—and for those
that can't stand
the plunge
there's the elevator
get your

Tattoo
on the
mezzanine.

Beneath this
bloody blackboard
(**smell** the bones of
Civil War dead) still
reeking the wind still
chalking the board in
brittle debate:
"Black and white—
Fight! Fight! Fight!"
or
"White and black—
Quack! Quick! Quack!"

Forget what's
above . . . it's
what's below we are
charged to know.
Jesus isn't looking
up, he is looking down
to the hurt, the halt
and the homo
and the 'ho,
and to the looting
headkicking
lame-o . . . not to a host
of heavenly habitants—

"If the habitants
of Heaven can't look
out for their own,"
J.C. figures, "tough shit
I got more pressing
needs below."
Stop looking up.
What? Are you still
thinking you can
kiss-ass

your way into winning
the lottery? Well
you better stock up
on a lot of
**PREPARATION H
LIP BALM!**
—if that's what
you think.

"That which is
against the way
will soon
cease to be."
—The Big Bood

KICKOUT

How did I get by with all these shenanigans under the gun? A reader might well wonder. I know I do, rambling through these obnoxious pages thirty years later. How did I keep these notes out of the guards' clammy hands? How did I get them all out of the San Mateo slammer when I was released?

Well, I didn't get them out. Good ol' pardner Page smuggled them past the kickout clerk in cutout compartments in his collection of hank books. A lot of the pages of the girlie mags were stuck together with some kinda nasty glue stuff. The clerk wrinkled his nose and shoved them under the glass with the rest of Page's personals.

The notebooks I tried to bring through disappeared. I saw them sitting on my probation officer's desk when I went in for my first interview. He didn't mention it and neither did I.

Page was the one that kept the books stashed while we were up at camp, too—in a big tome right on his nightstand. No skin mag, this book. A skin mag would have wandered off in the first horny hands that happened past. It was a hardbound of *Ashley's Book of Knots*, a leftover from Page's Navy days. It was always neatly knotted shut with a piece of real hemp line that he used for practice, sitting cross-legged on his bunk. When lights out was called he lashed the book up and secured the other end of the hemp line to his bunkframe.

"I ain't worried that the motherfuckers'll ever rip me for the book—they're too damn illiterate to appreciate what a classic *Ashley's* is worth. But some of them would jack the rope and try to smoke it."

I don't think I fully appreciated the book, either, until I got a look at it when he and I rendezvoused on the street. The last seven-eighths of the heavy pulp pages had been hacked out to make room for my burgeoning notes. Page said he had used the pages to paper the inside of his maintenance shop.

I did fully appreciate Page, though. A big ex–Shore Patrol Navy man with arms like hawsers and a face like a barnacle made a very valuable back-up in the lock-up.

I check in at the SM County facilities dressed in my usual stuff—leather jacket, striped pants and shoes, silver whistle hanging around my neck. They allow you to wear street business up at camp. The bulls here at County Slam hate the policy. Deputy Gerder looks up from his typewriter sees my outfit and his already stone-cold face freezes even harder.

"All right, Kesey. Give me everything."

"Everything?" Usually they let the Honor Camp prisoners check through, trust them to give up their watches, pocketknives, etc.

"Everything. We don't want you blowing your whistle at midnight."

"Make me out a complete property slip, then."

He gives me an unwavering stare through the mesh as he takes a triplicate form from a waiting stack and rolls it into the typewriter.

"One whistle," I say, pulling the chain over my head. "With a silver crucifix soldered to the side."

He doesn't type.

"One blues harp, E-flat."

He continues to look at me over the keys.

"Come on, Gerder; you want everything. I want a property slip for everything—whistles, harps, and all."

We both know what I'm really worried about are my two Honor Camp notebooks.

"You just slide everything into the trough," he says. "In fact, I want you out of that Davy Crockett costume, Jackoff. Peel it."

He comes out of the cage while I take off the fringed jacket Behema made me from the hide we skinned off the cow elk Cassady ran over coming down off Seven Devils Pass that All Souls' Eve with the brakes gone and the headlights blown.

"Stuff it in the trough. Now, hands on the wall feet on the line. Spread 'em." He gives the inside of my ankle a kick. "Deputy Rhack, back me while I examine this prisoner."

They frisk me. The whole shot, flashlight and all. Taking sunglasses, handkerchief, fingernail clippers, ballpoint pens and everything. My two notebooks are wrapped in the big farewell card Fassenaux drew for me on butcher paper. Gerder rips it off and stuffs it in the wastebasket. He tosses the notebooks on top of the other stuff.

"I get a property slip for this stuff, Gerder. That's the law."

"While you're in my tanks," Deputy Gerder lets me know, "you go by my law."

No malice in his voice. No anger. Just information.

"Okay then"—I take my two notebooks out of the trough and hold them up—"witness these." Showing them to Deputy Rhack and the rest of the men waiting in the receiving room. "Everybody? Two notebooks."

Then hand them to Gerder. He carries them around into his cage and sets them next to his typewriter. He hammers at the keys, ignoring the roomful of rancor across the counter from him. Rhack isn't so cool; a lot of these guys will be back up at camp with him for many months yet, where he's a guard without a gun. First he tries to oil us all with a wink, then he turns to me, smiling his sincerest man-to-man smile.

"So, Kesey . . . you think you got a book outta these six months with us?"

"I think so."

"How do you think it'll come out; in weekly installments in the *Chronicle*?"

"I hope not." Bonehead move, giving those three pages of notes to that Sunday supplement reporter—pulled my own covers. "It should make a book on its own."

"You'll have to change a lot, I'll bet . . . like the names."

"I'll bet a carton I don't. Sergeant *Rhack*? Deputy *Gerder*? Where can you come up with better names than those?"

Before Rhack can think up an answer Gerder jerks the papers out and slides them under the mesh. "Sign all three, Deputy."

Rhack has to use one of the pens from my pile. When Gerder gets the signed forms back he scoops all the little stuff out of the trough into a pasteboard property box with a numbered lid. He puts my wadded jacket on top.

"Okay, Kesey." He swivels to the panel of remote switches. "Zip up your pants and step to the gate."

"What about my notebooks?"

"You'll find stationery in Detain. Next."

Rhack hands me my ballpoint as I pass, and Gerder's right: there is paper in D Tank. Szikso is still here, too, after coming down for his kickout more than a week ago. In blues now instead of the flashy slacks and sportjacket, but still trying to keep up the cocky front, combing his greasy pomp, talking tough: "Good deal! The pussy wagon has arrived!"

One by one the other guys that rode down on Rhack's shuttle show up. Gerder has had to give them each the same treatment, taking cigarettes, paperbacks, everything.

"Sorry about that," I tell them.

"Steer clear of Kesey," Szikso advises them. "He's a heat magnet."

Just then keys jangle. "Kesey! Duggs is here to see you."

Door slides open. I follow the turnkey down the row of cells to a room with a desk. Probation Officer Duggs is sitting behind it. My two notebooks are on the desk beside my rapsheets. Duggs looks up from the records.

"I see you made it without getting any more Bad Time tacked on," Duggs says.

"I was good."

Duggs closes the folder. "Think anybody'll be here for you at midnight?"

"One of my family, probably."

"Down all the way from Oregon?"

"I hope so."

"Some family." He looks at me: caseworker look, conditioned sincere. Sympathetic. "Sorry about the report on your father."

"Thanks."

"That's why Judge Di Mateus waived that Bad Time, you know?"

"I know."

He lectures me awhile on the evils of blah blah blah. I let him run out his string. Finally he stands up, comes round the desk, sticks out his hand. "Okay, Short-timer. But don't miss the ten-thirty hearing Monday morning if you want to get released to an Oregon PO."

"I'll be here."

"I'll walk you back."

On the walk back to D Tank he asks what about this Jail Book; when will it be coming out? When it's over, I tell him. When might that be? When it stops happening.

Will this talk tonight be in it? Yes ... tonight, Monday morning, last week—everything will be in it.

"Kesey!" Szikso calls through the bars. "Put this in your fucking book: a guy—me—a guy shuns his comrades, plays pinochle five months with the motherfucking brass up there—five and a half months! When he musters down, one of those bulls misses a pack of Winstons and calls down and asks, 'What brand of cigarettes did Szikso check in with? Winstons? Slap a hold on him!' I mean is that cold or what, man? Is that a ballbusting bitch? But, what the fuck; Szikso will survive," he crows. "Felix Szikso is Sir Vivor!"

Some dudes can snivel so it sounds like they're crowing.

They lock me in and Duggs leaves. Szikso sits back down. He's doing Double Time, on hold like this—Now Time along with Street-to-Come Time. You can serve Triple Time, which adds on Street-gone-by Time and that is called Guilt. A man waiting for his kickout is on what's called Short Time. Short Time is known for being Hard Time. Lots of Short-timers go nuts or fuck up or try a run. Short is often harder than Long.

The best is Straight Time. That's what the notebooks are about.

More guys check in. Weekenders. D-Tankers. Some Blood hollers from the shadows, "Mercy, Deputy Dawg ... we done already *got* motherfuckers wall to wall ... "

Drunk tank full to overflowing
Motherfuckers wall to wall
Coming twice as fast as going
Time gets big; tank gets small

Dominoes slap on the table
Bloods play bones in tank next door
Bust a bone, if you be able
Red Death* stick it good some more.

Three days past my kickout time
Ask to phone; don't get the juice—
Crime times crime just equals more crime
Cut the motherfuckers loose.

Will I make the Christmas kickout?
Will commissary come today?
Will they take my blood for Good Time
Or just take my guts away?

*Red Death. What they call the glop of strawberry jelly comes with breakfast coffee and toast—makes, among other things, quite a powerful glue.

Some snitch found my homemade outfit!
They've staked a bull up at the still!
They've scoped the pot plants we were sprouting
At the bottom of the hill.

They punched my button, pulled my covers
Blew my cool, ruint my ruse
They've rehabilitated this boy
Cut this motherfucker loose.

The fish that nibbles on the wishing
Let him off his heavy rod
The gowned gavel-bangers fishing
Cut them loose from playing God.

Back off Johnson, back off peacefreaks
From vendettas, from Vietnam
Cut loose the squares, cut loose the hippies
Cut loose the dove, cut loose the bomb.

You, the finger on the trigger
You, the hand that weaves the noose
You hold the blade of brutal freedom —
Cut all the motherfuckers loose.

Eleven-forty they take me out give me my clothes whistle and harp put me in this room with a bench and one other Short-timer, gray-pated mahogany-hued old dude of sixty years or so.

"Oh, am I one Ready Freddy. Am I ever!"

He's pacing around the little room picking up and putting back down and picking back up one of those old-fashioned footrest shoeshine kits, full of personals. He has on a worn black suit, maroon tie and white shirt. His shoes have a sensational shine.

"What you in for, Home?"

"Weed. What about you?"

"I pull a knife on my brother-in-law ... my old woman call the cops. Wasn't no actual goddamn fight whatsoever. But I don't care. Just let me get on my mother *way*!"

Putting down his kit sipping his coffee picking his kit back up.

"Yessir, on my *way*!"

"Good luck on it," I say.

"Same to you. Ah, I don't care. I even lost some weight in here. Met some nice folks, too. . . ."

A young black trusty stops in and gives him a number on a slip of paper.

"I hope you writ where I can read it," the old man says.

"Plenty big, Pop. Don't forget. Call soon as you hit a phone, tell her her *Sugardog* still be barkin'."

"I'll do it. I sure will!"

"Thanks, Pop. Be cool."

As soon as the kid is gone the old man wads the paper and drops it in the pisser.

"Damn fool tramp. Met some real motherfuckers, too, as you can see." He puts the kit down so he can rub his hands as he paces. "Oh, that ol' city be just right, Saturday night still cookin'. If I can get me to a bus, that is. What's the time?"

"I got twelve straight up. I should have some family waiting; we'll give you a lift."

"Appreciate it," he says. "Straight up you tell me? Ah well, I don't care. We got nothin but time to do, wher*ever* we be. What you say you been in on?"

"Possession."

"If that ain't a shame—for the good green gift of the Lord. He hadn't wanted it to grow, there wouldna been seeds. How much they give you?"

"Six months, five-hundred-dollar fine, three-year tail."

"If that ain't the shits."

"It's done."

"I reckon. Nothin but time—" He starts to take a sip of his cold coffee, stops—"'ceptin, oh, I am *ready*."

He puts the cup down, picks the kit back up.

"Franklin!" a voice calls. "William O.—"

"In the wind, Boss. On my way!"

I'm alone on the bench, sipping what's left of his cup of coffee, spoon still sticking out. The plastic bag his suit was in hangs from the conduit; his blues are right where he left them, on the floor. Ghost clothes. I'm ready too. This stationery is finished both sides.

"Kesey! Ken E.—"

"On my way!"